From Beginner

to

Soccer Superstar

Soccer Drills for Kids Ages 6 - 10

Chest Dugger

Table of Contents

About the Author

Chest Dugger is a soccer fan, former professional and coach now looking to share his knowledge. Enjoy this book and several others that he has written.

Here is the link to the other books he has written.

https://www.amazon.com/stores/Chest-Dugger/author/B0BWSKLCNX

Free Gift Included

As part of our dedication to help you succeed in your career, we have sent you a free soccer drills worksheet, known as the "Soccer Training Work Sheet" drill sheet. The worksheet is a list of drills that you can use to improve your game and a methodology to track your performance on these drills on a day-to-day basis. We want to get you to the next level.

Click on the link below to get your free drills worksheet.

https://soccertrainingabiprod.gr8.com/

Disclaimer

Copyright © 2026

All Rights Reserved

No part of this eBook can be transmitted or reproduced in any form including print, electronic, photocopying, scanning, mechanical, or recording without prior written permission from the author.

While the author has taken the utmost effort to ensure the accuracy of the written content, all readers are advised to follow information mentioned herein at their own risk. The author cannot be held responsible for any personal or commercial damage caused by the information herein. All readers are encouraged to seek professional advice when needed.

Introduction

When adults hear the word "superstar," they often imagine famous professional players performing in packed stadiums. But for young children learning the game, the meaning is very different. A soccer superstar at age six to ten is not defined by trophies, goals, or fame. A true young superstar is simply a player who loves the game, feels confident with the ball, enjoys practicing new skills, and plays with enthusiasm. Every great player begins as a beginner. The purpose of this book is to help young players develop the skills, confidence, and love for soccer that can turn them into their own version of a soccer superstar.

It takes a special kind of coach to work with under sixes, under eights, under nines and under tens. Coaching children as young as this brings about many rewards but does require a number of traits and a good deal of understanding about how young children learn and acquire their own skills. Maybe prime amongst these special requirements is patience. Let us explain. Most likely, we are coaching soccer because we love the sport. Maybe we have a daughter or a son who has joined a club; most probably the secretary of that club is on the lookout for keen coaches. And again, most probably the ages groups without a dedicated coach are the youngest ones, because they are the trickiest to teach.

THE 5 SIGNS OF A YOUNG SUPERSTAR

1. Loves having the ball at their feet

2. Tries new moves and skills

3. Helps their teammates

4. Plays with energy and confidence

5. Has fun every time they step on the field

It helps to have good people skills if we are coaching fellow adults. This is even more the case if we are working with teenagers, and again with under twelves, elevens or tens. But if these people orientated skills are invaluable with these age groups, they are essential if we are coaching under sixes, sevens or eights.

To return to the fact that prime among the wide range of personal we will require is patience: it is unlikely that we have taken on a coaching role with no knowledge of the sport, but we are working with young people who themselves will have little concept of the nature of the sport. Many will need to acquire such rudimentary skills as kicking the ball or running with it. Many more will have effectively no understanding of space or teamwork. It will be the rare eight year old (and even rarer in among the other children covered by the scope of this book) who has any concept of the unfolding nature of a game of soccer, the nuances and intricacies of the game.

Not that this really matters, because although soccer at the highest level is one of the most tactical, skilled and evolved sports on the planet, it is also, at its core, among the simplest. But for all that, it is important to understand where young players are in their personal development. To have a theoretical knowledge of why concepts which seem unquestionable to us – the value of passing to a teammate for example – may be unfathomable to them. It is the limits of young children's stages of emotional, cognitive, physical and conceptual development with which we have to work, and also which require both our extreme patience, and (more than any other age group we might ever coach, right up to veterans) our understanding.

Because in much the same way that we cannot make an eighteen year old lad understand the risks of certain behaviours – the frontal cortex is insufficiently developed compared to the rest of their brain – so we cannot in any significant way impact the personal development of the young children with which we are working. We can help, we can model and we can shape, but whatever our skills just as we cannot make a full size Venus De Milo out of a small pot of plasticine; similarly we cannot make a Lionel Messi or a Kevin De Bruyne out of a small pot of player. Crucially, nor should we try. We work with what we have, recognising that our players are at quite different stages of their development, and that it is important to factor this into our expectations. Our goals are to allow our children to progress at their own speed, celebrating them for what they are whilst not trying to impart knowledge, skills or concepts which are simply beyond their stages of development.

That, in a nutshell, is the philosophy behind this coaching book. The drills and information over the coming pages take as their premise the notion that the child is at the centre of what we do. In educationalist terms, it is a child-centred approach. We take what the child can do, can understand and will enjoy as the basis for moulding these attributes into ones which will be useful to them as budding soccer players.

Child Protection

We will take a brief diversion here to look at two important factors which every coach (who works with any age of young person) really needs to consider. This is also for their own protection. There is a podcast on the BBC called 'My Mate's a Footballer'. If it is available in your region, then it is highly recommended as a brilliant way to provide an entertaining forty five minutes a week. It features a comedian, Joe Wilkinson (very funny, in a dry, self-deprecating kind of way) interviewing a former England international and Premier League soccer player, Patrick Bamford. Bamford is now in the second tier with Leeds United, but they seem on track, at the time of writing, to ascend back to the Premier League. The premise is that Wilkinson wants to get to know Bamford and his life as a professional soccer player in order to become his friend. It really is very entertaining, and quite fascinating for soccer fans as Bamford offers insights to many of the aspects of being a professional which we, as fans, do not know. Matters such as the team surrounding him (he has a personal fitness trainer, a mental health advisor and a chef, for example). However, in one episode, the player mentions that Child Protection rules are so tight that a seventeen year old player who has broken into the first team is not permitted to change with the other, adult, players.

If that is the level of Child Protection in professional soccer, then it will be extremely tight at the level of under six play, and indeed right through the youth age ranges. Each club will have its own policies, which must be followed, but it is strongly recommended that coaches always work with a second adult present. Many of the drills to follow include a second coach, often to keep players busy while the head coach works with individuals or small, rotating, groups. It is likely that most clubs will have the presence of a second adult listed in their child protection protocols, but this might be simply two age groups working in close proximity of each other.

If a second, assistant coach, cannot be found, most parents will agree to attending sessions on a rotating basis, providing that assurance for the coach.

Dealing with Parents

In their enthusiasm to support you, as their much loved coach, the team and their child (as hard as this is to believe) sometimes parents can get a tiny bit out of control. They've even been known to shout abuse, in their moment of temporary enthusiasm, at other players, opposing parents, you as the coach, the referee and at times, at their own little Johnny.

Actually, the above is not true. This unwanted behaviour is not temporary enthusiasm, parents who display the worst of these anti-social acts are over competitive louts who should not be permitted within a hundred metres of their child's soccer pitch. It is usually, but not always, dads, and they are vicariously living their own thwarted dreams through their young son or (less often, in this scenario) daughter. They clearly lack the basic understanding and decency to understand that they are not watching professional soccer played, coached and refereed by high earning adults.

Still, that statement of the obvious does not remove them from the soccer playing equation. Clubs should include a statement of behaviour in their policies and protocols to which parents must sign up. A zero tolerance policy is recommended, with occasional 'silent support' games, where only applause is permitted from spectators, as a reminder when some followers are getting out of control.

There is no place in youth soccer, in any scenario, for disparaging comments, for abuse and for aggressive behaviour. As coaches we have our own duty to ourselves, to our (unpaid) referees and mostly to our young players to stop poor behaviour from parents. If parents will not listen, then it is perfectly right to exclude them.

What does a Child Centred Approach Look Like?

Earlier, the philosophy behind this book is identified as a child centred one. It may be useful to explain how this will work. In broad terms, our philosophy is split into two categories: what we will seek to improve among our players, and what we won't. Because the list is shorter, we will begin with the second of these.

What Will We Not Look to Coach?

Tactics. There will be no work on set plays, on formations or on high presses, mid-blocks and low blocks. Children of the age with which we are working have short concentration spans. They have boundless enthusiasm, but not for tactics. Their enthusiasm is for running around, kicking a ball and having fun.

Winning. Whether you are based in the States, or Australia, or South Africa, or Europe or anywhere in the world, you will know that soccer has its modern routes in Britain, when the FA was formed back in the mid-1800s, the game had developed from the Public Schools and into the industrialising regions of the North of England. (Actually, the soccer most probably originated many thousands of years ago in China, or possible – although this is much debated – even further back among the Aborigine peoples in Australia – but these are other stories, interesting ones, but not within the scope of this coaching book.)

So given that historically the modern game originated in the UK, and is an obsession in England and Scotland at least, one may wonder why, for so many years, these nations were so terrible at the game. The answer lies in an obsession among youth soccer coaches for winning. Right down to the youngest age groups. So how do you get a group of ten year old boys (girls? Dream on, in those dark days of the sixties, seventies and eighties) to win against another set ten year old boys?

Simple.

You put your biggest player at the back and told him to hoof it forward as far as he can, on the huge pitches filled with twenty-two small and lost souls. Meanwhile, your quickest player was up front, and he used his pace to chase the long kick, outrun the lumbering defenders, and score (in the large goals which dwarfed their tiny goalkeepers.) While the dinosaurs who held sway in the English game refused to change, European nations such as Spain, Italy and Germany were developing small sided, small pitch systems which allowed all children to develop their skills, so that by the time the players reached their early teens, and began to become more even developmentally advanced, there was a large pool of highly talented players still involved in the game. It took the forward thinking former international Trevor Brooking to force through changes to the youth and children's game, and my, was he unpopular for doing so?

Fortunately, these days just about everybody understands that for young children, winning is merely a by-product of helping them to become technically, mentally and physically better players. Plus, returning to our understanding of child development, rarely are children of the age with whom we are working themselves terribly interested in victory. Where they are, this is normally a reflection of their own parents' motivations.

If tactics and winning are two aspects of soccer on which we are not focussed in this manual, then let us spend a while looking at the facets of the game which will inform our focus.

Areas on which we do focus in the coming pages

Acquisition of skills. We will provide drills and tips to help our young players become more able in key individual skills. In particular, we will look at the vital aspects of the game of passing, including receiving the pass, dribbling and shooting. We will seek to help coaches instil in their charges good technique but do so by using our players' own developmental stage – their enthusiasm and desire to be active in particular – to enhance these techniques and skills. Thus, only rarely do we suggest drills which directly help to establish, improve and ingrain technique. Instead, in line with the interests and enjoyment of the players, we will offer lots of games and highly energetic activities which will in turn help our players to acquire and improve their technique.

Improvement in agility. As coaches, we must accept that the coordination of our players is still very much in development. It will also be extremely variable between players in our group. We will have youngsters capable of quite complex agility skills such as stepovers and turns, whilst many others simply will not be coordinated enough to do this. Inevitably, our response to dealing with this variety in development comes back to our long term aim of seeing the best opportunity of improvement in all of our players. After all, if we were concerned solely about winning, then Amelia, who can turn on a sixpence, and Jordan, who can step over with both feet, would probably make our line-up, although when it comes to seeking victory at all costs, neither is likely to be as effective as the child who can kick the ball half the length of the pitch. By the under ten stage, the situation will be much changed, and Amelia and Jordan are likely to be the most effective players on the pitch…except, if they have not had much practice, or much encouragement, because we have simply looked to win by hoofing the ball up field, they are most probably lost to the game. And if they are lost, then the children who, aged six, were still at earlier points in their physical development would be long gone from the soccer world. So, we look to encourage and improve every player, taking into account their starting points.

However, it cannot be denied that the considerable differences in natural ability and development evident with young children can make coaching difficult. Our best answer is to set each child slightly varied challenges within the structure of the drill. To illustrate this point, let us use **Drill on Narrow Spaces** in Page 58 as an example. While most children might undertake the drill as set, for Jordan and Amelia, with their advanced skills, we might as coach, offer a little semi opposition as they are dribbling through the narrowing lines of cones. We do not have design entire programmes for each child, just make small tinkerings which will allow each player to succeed as far as they can.

Teamwork. This is an important aspect of the game. In the final chapter, Off the Field Development, we talk a little about our players' stage of development. Particularly at the youngest age range covered by the book, our players will only just be beginning to move from the developmental stage of egocentricity towards more wide ranging social interaction. Some of our players will still firmly be within the egocentric stage. This is not a criticism of them, nor is it something we can particularly look to change. Egocentricity is a normal stage of child development. Fundamentally, it means that children are still seeing the world overwhelmingly from their own perspective. They are central to their world, and their empathy towards others is something that is still to develop. Most probably, it emerges from the vulnerability of young children, particularly as a part of a large family group (as would typically be the case historically) and the need of child to promote their own interests, particularly in terms of their parents, over those of their peers and siblings. In the modern world, where in developed nations that vulnerability is much, much less than it used to be, this developmental stage shows itself in a lack of awareness of the needs and interests of others. Most children grow out of the stage quite quickly, and by the time our players reach the age to be part of an under eight squad, they are much more highly attuned to the needs and interests of their peers – indeed, they now begin to seek social acceptance amongst their peers, allowing the soccer coaching of them (or indeed any kind of teaching) to become much easier, something that will continue to improve as they get older, probably right up to their mid-teens when youngsters can once more become challenging to work with, albeit for very different reasons.

But where we are working with children at the egocentric stage of development, we cannot force them out of it. Instead, we need to work within this stage, showing, for example, how sharing can lead to personal reward. In practical terms, stickers or other prizes can be very motivating for young children, and help to shape their behaviour, teaching them self-motivation to improve teamwork. Albeit very slowly.

Pace of sessions. The old Chinese proverb says, 'I hear and I forget, I see and I remember, I do and I understand.' It may have been around for a long time, but should be ingrained on every teacher's, and therefore every coach's, soul. When working with young children an additional phrase is needed. 'I run around a lot and I improve.' One of the key tenets of this book is to keep our players busy and active. As coaches of young children we aim to keep explanations to an absolute minimum. If we need to give a demonstration, we make it quick and engaging (involving as many senses as possible, throwing in verbal gags for example, to help the players remain engaged). We keep drills simple so that explanations can be minimal. If a drill is more complicated, because there is no alternative, we break it down rather than try to include the entire drill in one explanation. As soon as it is possible to do so, we get our players running about. That way, not only do they learn more effectively, but they remain interested. As any parent knows, a bored six year old is not an easy child with whom to deal. It we have a group of twelve bored six year olds, we have a big problem on our hands.

Enjoyment. Although saved to last, this is perhaps the most important aspect which drives the philosophy of this book. We seek to offer an enjoyment of soccer to our young players. There are many reasons for this, perhaps most important of them being that it is just right that our players enjoy their soccer. In addition, if they arrive looking forward to their session, they are likely to be easier to manage. They will learn more quickly because they will be motivated to do so. They become far more likely to stick with the sport, and equally are more encouraged to try other sports, which is a good thing.

They will also develop better relationships, have more self-confidence, be better prepared to cope with success and failure, because neither will matter so much if they are having fun whatever, perform better academically, become more popular and more socially aware older children and adults.

Indeed, the importance of having fun cannot be overstated. Being the coach of a soccer team, especially a youth or children's team, offers such a great opportunity to players to have fun. For us as coaches, that we are enabling our young soccer players to have such fun is surely the most rewarding aspect of what we do. Coaching also offers the chance to do so much good. And this is a responsibility in which we must do our best to achieve as well as we can for our charges. If that is the philosophy we hold, to provide opportunities for fun to our players, within a sporting and social environment, then not only will we be good coaches, but we will be helping children and young people in so many aspects of their lives. Both now, and in the years to come.

Certainly, very young children are the most difficult to coach. But when we succeed, they also are most unsubtle at showing their pleasure and their appreciation. And we all like to receive that. Whoever we are.

Key to Drills

Each of the following thirty drills, activities and tips (along with games) include diagrams. They have been used to help with clarity in setting up and ease of understanding the operation of the drills. In these diagrams, the following symbols are used:

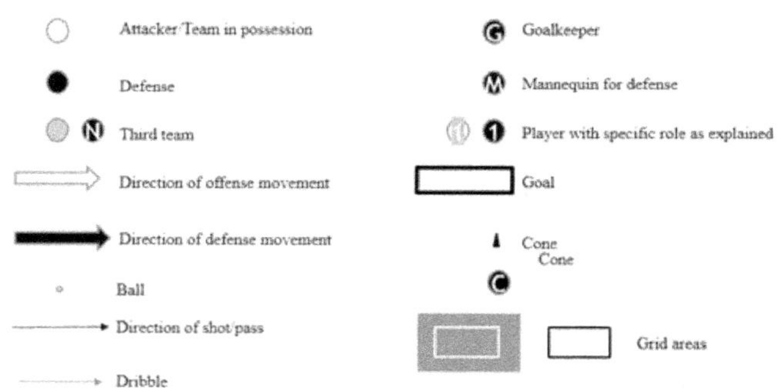

There are specific explanations of symbols by some drills, this being where they differ from or are not included among the main symbols used. Please note that the diagrams are not drawn to scale.

LEVEL 1 – GETTING COMFORTABLE ON THE FIELD

Spatial Awareness

Spatial awareness is one of those terms often bandied about, especially in the field of sports. Without, perhaps, a full understanding of what the phrase actually means. How often do we hear a commentator in a key soccer match state, with no apparent sense of irony, 'He has his back to goal but knows exactly where the posts are to be found', or words to that effect? As former England International and Golden Boot winner turned presenter Gary Lineker once replied: 'Well, the goalposts don't move.'

But the ball does, opponents do and, most crucially for young children, so do they. That ability to understand their own position with regards to other objects, both ones that are stationary, and those that move around, is what we mean when using the term spatial awareness.

As we have already alluded, much of the challenge in working with children aged six to ten – maybe also younger ones as well – comes in melding our teaching of the skills, techniques and flow of the game of soccer to our players' stage of development. Like so much, we cannot instil in our players complete spatial awareness; they will get it when they get it. Many of us will have inwardly smiled at the sight of a young player tearing off down the pitch, making huge progress – a testament to their developing dribbling skills – their teammates hollering as loud as they can. Just, the player is running in the wrong direction. And their teammates' shouts are not ones of encouragement but instructions to turn round. That is a lack of spatial awareness in very visual play. However, we can offer opportunities for this developmental stage to hasten towards improvement. Children gather their sense of spatial awareness through play, because that is the way they experience the world, and build relationships. To help them progress we will need to use play – games – in our coaching.

But although we cannot do much more than to provide opportunities to develop this awareness – it is not something we can teach, as we might the technique of shooting with the laces or doing a Cruyff turn – it is important to understand why it is something which children will need to acquire as a part of their own developmental process.

There is much research which links spatial awareness to cognitive development. Fine motor skills develop as a result of spatial awareness – to use a simple example, children cannot develop the coordination required to pick up a pencil, let alone use it, without understanding the relationship between the position of that pencil and themselves. Spatial awareness also tells us where our teammates are, where opponents are placed, and the direction they are moving both in relation to ourselves, and where we wish to pass the ball. To return to the Gary Lineker anecdote, mentioned above, it is their spatial awareness that will tell older players where to place a shot when it is made on the turn, starting with their back to goal. So, perhaps those commentators are not quite as daft as they sound… (Joking…of course they are.)

Their spatial awareness will also help children to develop relationships, to share and enjoy playing with friends. It's growth in an individual helps them to move from the stage of egocentricity towards a more empathetic view of their world. As will be the case so often in this book, when we help young children acquire a particular skill, or attitude or, as in this case, awareness, we are not only helping them to become better soccer players, but also more successful people, confident of their place among their peers. This is what sport can do, and why, as coaches, we are so privileged and important to helping that process.

Soccer Drill: Chasing Shadows

This is a fun warm up game which doesn't involve a ball, but gets our players running around, and developing a sense of spatial awareness through movement, speed and cognizance of others. The competitive element is developed through players attempting to avoid the 'shadow', working with team mates to avoid capture. (Note – we do not often add a competitiveness element to our drills, and if this feels uncomfortable for your group, simply do not focus on it.). Games without a ball do have a valuable use with younger players, because the addition of the ball can often become a challenge to children aged between six and ten which detracts from other aspects of their development as a player. It makes the core objective of the drill harder to achieve. Therefore, by removing the ball from the equation, it is possible to focus on whatever skill or technique is being practised. Of course, though, soccer is a ball sport, so we should still ensure that the vast majority of our sessions involve a ball.

Use With: Any age, this game will work well right up to Under 13s, but young children love the fun element of it.

Objectives: Avoid capture by releasing new 'shadows'. Develop spatial awareness by reaching correct areas and avoiding contact with others.

Equipment: This is incredibly simple to set up. Simply mark out 10 metres by 10 metres grid (adapting size to the number of players taking part). It is an ideal 'first activity' – lively, fun and engaging. Perfect for one coach to lead whilst another sets up the more complex, soccer based activities and drills for later in the session.

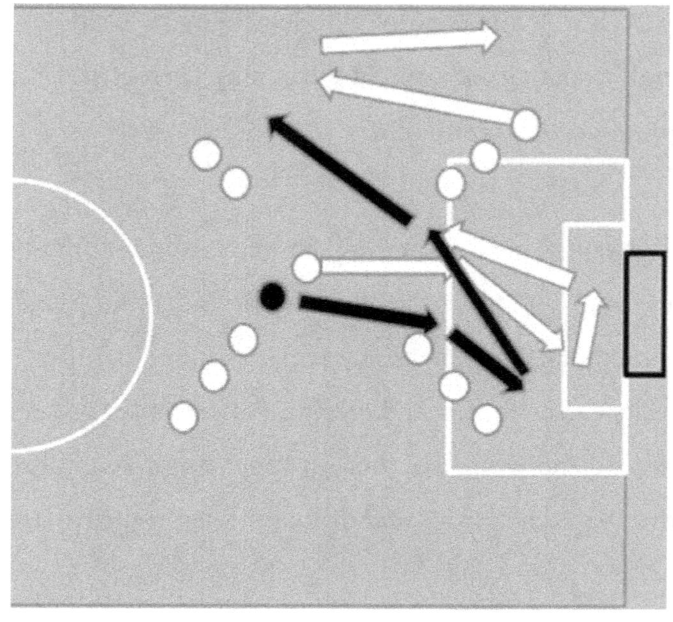

The diagram above is shown without the grid, and this is simply because there is a great deal of movement in the drill, and to show this in a limited space would be hard to achieve. The diagram illustrates the black dot (chaser) chasing the white dot (shadow) closest to them. The white dot dodges to the front of a set of three players, and the rearmost then becomes the one being chased.

Operation of Drill:

- Divide the players into four equal groups.

- Choose one player from one of the groups to act as the 'chaser', another player from another group to be the 'shadow'.

- Line up the remain players facing inwards on the four points of the compass, that is, at right angles to each other.

- Separate the chaser and the shadow. Say 'Go', and the chaser must try to 'tag' the shadow.

- If they succeed, direct the shadow to the front of any line, the player at the back of the line becomes the new shadow.

- The shadow can release a new shadow at any time by moving to the front of any line. The player at the back then becomes the new shadow.

- Swap the chaser every couple of minutes.

- Play for 6-8 minutes.

- Note: there is a bit of standing around involved, although players will enjoy the chase so are

unlikely to become bored. However, if training
outdoors on a chilly evening, keep the game short.

Key Skills:

- Agility and movement to catch or chase.
- Judgement as to when to release a new shadow.

Development:

- Add a ball.
- Now the game becomes about tackling rather than
  tagging.
- The shadow can release a new shadow by passing to
  a player at the back of a line of teammates. They then
  become the new shadow.
- When the shadow passes, he or she moves to the
  front of the line to which they have passed.

Soccer Drill: Moving Lines

Another fast and furious activity which does not involve a ball. Player involvement is increased here, and again there is a fun element which keeps players entertained and focussed on the session.

Use With: Any age, but this activity works particularly well with largish groups.

Objectives: Develop spatial awareness by moving quickly and strategically to avoid being tagged.

Equipment: As with Chasing Shadows, this is a very simple activity to set up. No equipment is needed, as the players themselves become the obstacles around or through which the chaser and their target operate.

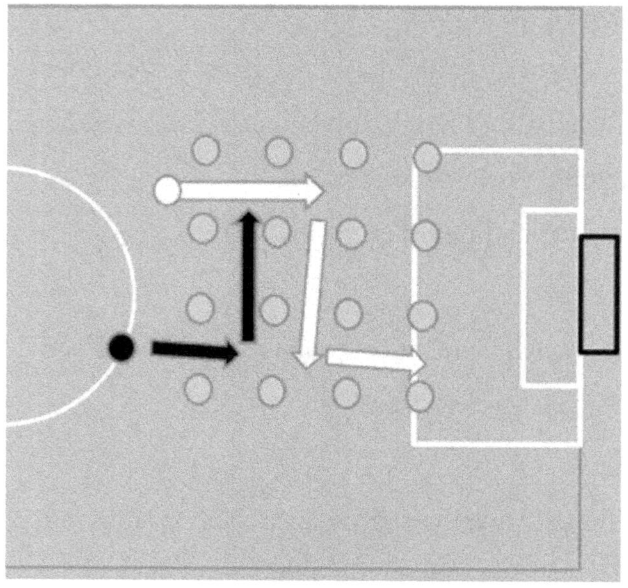

Operation of Drill:

- Divide the players into groups of four or five.

- Line the players up and tell them to shuffle until they are an arm's length from the player in front. Get them to touch their team mate on the shoulder to help them to understand how far an arm's length actually is.

- Now get them to repeat the activity with the player to their left.
- There are three instructions:
  - DOWN – on this instruction, players let both arms drop to their sides.
  - SIDE – here, players reach out with their left arm and rest their hand on a teammate's shoulder. (Check players know their left from their right.)
  - FORWARD – on this instruction, players reach forward to rest on a teammate's shoulder.
- Choose two players from the front or back row.
- One is the chaser, the other the target.
- Place these players inside the lines, at opposite corners.
- Starting with the 'DOWN' instruction, the chaser must navigate through the players and tag the target, who must try to avoid being tagged.

- At various points, shout one of the instructions
  FORWARD and SIDE. Channels are created, and
  players must use these channels to run in.
- On capture, or when the target has evaded being
  tagged for long enough, choose two more players,
  replacing them in their lines with the previous
  chaser and target.

Key Skills:

- Coordination to change direction quickly to run
  through teammates.
- Strategy on the move to plan routes to avoid capture
  or tag the target.

Development:

- With large groups, have two or even three targets and
  chasers.

Soccer Drill: Changing Pitches

The final warm up activity in this section does involve a ball. It builds on the Moving Lines drill above. However, it is a dribbling and scoring activity rather than a chasing one.

Use With: Any age, although inexperienced six year olds will find the changing of directions quite difficult to begin with.

Objectives: Dribble around and through players, developing spatial awareness through movement and changes in direction around objects (i.e., their teammates.)

Equipment: Bibs, four small goals, four balls.

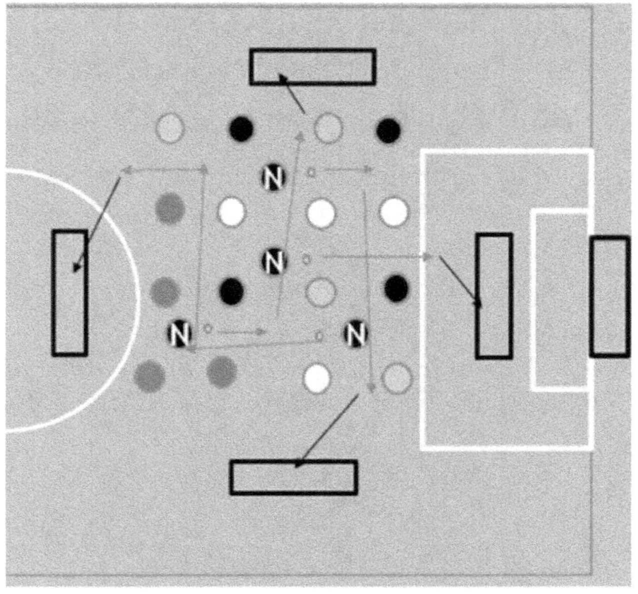

Operation of Drill:

In the diagram above the coach has firstly positioned the four teams who make up the channels through which players from the fourth team will dribble. These teams are represented by the black, white, light grey and dark grey circles. The dribbling team are represented by the 'N' team.

- Set up the activity as for Moving Lines above.

- When players are in position hand out some coloured bibs so that there are three or four players in each colour.

- When setting up, keep one of the teams out of the grid as this will make resetting easier for them later. This is the team which will be first to undertake the activity.

- Place a goal at each point of the compass outside of the player lines.

- Allocate one of the four goals to each of the four players about to dribble.

- Start the players opposite their goals.

- On the instruction 'GO', players must dribble within the grid of teammates, avoiding where possible touching a teammate. Shout directions in line with the Moving Lines activity, creating channels through which players must dribble.

- After a minute or so, shout 'GOAL'. Now the players must dribble and score in their own goals, (it you wish to add a competitive element, say first to do so wins.)

- Extra fun can be added by continuing to shout the other instructions, meaning a player headed for their goal might suddenly find their pathway blocked. However, judge this, and whether there will be a 'winner', on your knowledge of your group. Some younger children find losing difficult to cope with, especially if they feel they are about to score when the grid changes. They will see this as unfair, and there is little more developed in a seven year old than their sense of fairness. Whilst losing is a vital lesson to learn, a session can deteriorate quickly if players lose their self-control.

Key Skills:

- Dribbling and changing direction with the ball.
- Planning a route to goal.

Development:

- Add a tackler.

- If the tackler ends up in the same channel as a player with the ball, the channel will be too narrow for the dribbler to pass, so they must learn to shield the ball until the channels change again.

Soccer Drill: Touch and Pass

A fast-paced drill which helps players learn how to work out the position of opponents, and also the position of the goal when their back is to it.

Use With: Any age. Younger children will require more touches and a shorter distance between the various elements of the drill.

Objectives: A number of objectives here which help to develop spatial awareness. Locating the position of defenders is the key objective, however players will also develop the skill of passing backwards, away from goal, which is a tactic which will need be taught as young children tend to head automatically towards the goal, rather than use the space on the pitch to create opportunities.

The drill also helps them to improve their sense of where the goal is, when they prepare to shoot having had their backs to it.

Equipment: Several balls. Goal. Three mannequins (or coaches/players) but mannequins definitely work best.

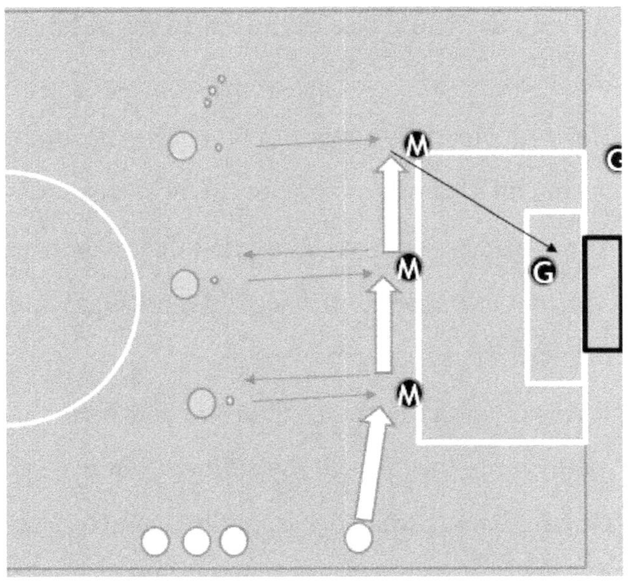

Operation of Drill: There are various elements to the drill. A pair of goalkeepers to alternate ready to save shots. Three feeders who will pass the ball into their teammates (these players each have a ball, the spare balls are placed near to the final feeder). Three mannequins or defenders. The remaining players prepare to undertake the drill.

- Player one (white circle) runs in front of the first defender.

- He or she reaches behind to touch the mannequin, giving an idea of the position of the defender.

- The feeder passes into them, and they pass back.

- The player runs onto the second mannequin, and the activity is repeated.

- When the player reaches the third and final mannequin, they repeat the activity, but instead of passing back, turn away from the mannequin and attempt to score. Allow touches dependent on the age and skill level of the player.

- The activity can flow easily. Start the next player as soon as the previous player reaches the middle mannequin.

- Once they have had their shot, players run around to the back of the line, ready to go again.

- Goalkeepers swap after every shot.

- Spare keeper returns the ball, to ensure that there is a ready supply for the final feeder.

- After a while, swap the feeders.

Key Skills:

- Identifying the position of the defender.

- Receiving the pass with a good first touch.

- Passing backwards, away from goal.

- Turning and shooting when they have had their backs to goal.

- Goalkeeping to save shots from an angle.

Development:

- Place an active defender in the third position.

- This player can try to win the ball.

- If this is a coach, they can work out how much opposition to offer to ensure that players still get some success.

Soccer Drill: Space Game

A game where the intention is to teach our young players the value of finding space. The drill partly takes advantage of the concept in netball where players are permitted only in designated areas of the pitch. The game also uses rondo style techniques, with play weighted towards attack.

Use With: Any age. Keep the pitches small but designate the size dependent on the age and skill level of the players, with smaller pitches for less experienced players.

Objectives: To understand that finding space is more important than chasing the ball, thus developing a sense of spatial awareness of the pitch. Beyond that, the drill is a game type scenario, with the scoring of goals the objective to which players are motivated.

Equipment: Small pitch marked out with zones.

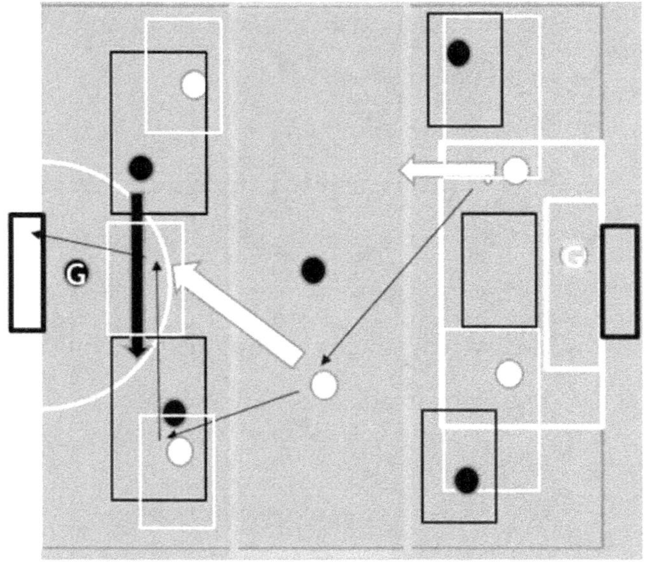

(In the diagram above, the grey box in the middle is the midfield area for both teams, the other boxes represent the zones for each team, white boxes for the white team and black boxes for the black team.)

Operation of Drill:

- The Pitch

- Normal pitch, with goals at either end, but small and marked out in zones.
  - There are three attacking zones, a wide midfield zone, and two defensive zones.
  - There is some overlap in the offensive and defensive zones.
  - Ideally play six a side, but the game does work up to nine a side.
- The Players
  - The goalkeeper is allowed only in their area.
  - Two defenders can go in either of the two defensive zones. This means that both defenders could be in the same zone at the same time, which will help children learn about space as the opposite attacker will be left unmarked. In crossing from one defensive zone to the other, the player cannot remain in the central attacking zone, nor interfere with play in any way.
  - One defender at a time can enter the midfield zone.

- o The midfielder can enter the midfield and any attacking zones.
  - o The strikers can each only stay in their designated wide zone.
  - o This should create 3 v 2 attacking situations
  - o These are quite complicated instructions. We suggest delivering to each group – defenders, goalkeepers, strikers etc separately one at a time. The players will pick up what to do when they play – 'I do and I understand'! but it may take a couple of tries.
  - o With more players, allocate players to a specific zone, although it is important that the midfielders can also attack in order to create the overload necessary for the game.
- The Game
  - o Keep the games fairly short, as players may become frustrated if they do not receive enough of the ball.
  - o Change positions regularly.
  - o The temptation will be to put the best players in the midfield spots, as these are the most

influential on the game. However, try to avoid this as the best players will naturally draw passes and still have an influence on the game. Although their spatial awareness is likely to be better than that of their peers, they still need to learn the skills, plus by placing less able players in the midfield roles they will have an opportunity to play a match where they can get on the ball with less pressure.

Key Skills:

- Holding a position rather than chasing the ball.
- Passing as this gets the ball to goal scoring positions most quickly.
- Learning the importance of positioning on the pitch

Development:

- Introduce the idea of defenders attacking wide space by allowing defenders to enter their wide attacking zone

- If the concepts do not become too complicated, allow strikers to enter the central attacking zone, creating overloads in this area.

- As players' skills and concepts of space improve, allow overlapping of zones.

- Gradually reduce the number of zones, making them larger, until eventually there are just four overlapping zones. If the players have learnt positional sense, they will still seek space, using their spatial awareness to adopt the best positions. If they return to 'honeypot' ball chasing, reintroduce zones.

This is quite a complex game, but more so for the coach than the players. Largely, our players need only to remember the zones they can enter and this is quite closely defined. When using the drill for the first time it is recommended that the playing area be set up in advance, as it can be quite time consuming, and that the coach ensures they are clear in their own minds the rules and limits of the drill.

In summary, it is important to remember that spatial awareness is a developmental stage in young children, much more so than a sporting one. Whilst we can aid their development, make it easier for them to understand the spaces around them, and their relationship to those spaces and to other players, as coaches we should not become frustrated if progress is slow. That will be only because the children are young and is neither a reflection on their efforts nor on our coaching skills.

Reward 2:

As a reward for reading this chapter on tactical awareness, we wanted to give you a bonus that you will enjoy. It's a book on Soccer Intelligence that looks at different skills and strategies to improve a player's awareness on the field. Just scan the QR code below to get your book.

Building Coordination and Agility

What do we mean by coordination and agility? Most of us will have a broad, but not necessarily completely correct notion of what these terms mean. Indeed, in researching this book, we found ourselves nodding with enlightenment as we absorbed new information, and smiling as this information made such obvious sense.

So let us start with agility. By which we mean (certainly within the context of young children) balance. Specifically, the ability to retain balance whilst placing our body in unusual positions. Running with a ball at our feet is not a normal human action, dropping our shoulder to change direction then dodging the other way is equally not a normal set of actions. But both are something that, say, wingers, indeed all soccer players, learn to use as they progress in the game. The ability to do this at speed and without falling over is an example of agility. The element of the process which stops us from falling over is our balance.

Balance is developed in part through our use of senses, for example our eyes help us to see where we are in relation to the ground, our ears the proximity of teammates and opponents. The more we practice using our senses with our body in different positions, the better we get at balance. The more agile we become. But balance is also a physiological process, with fluid in our inner ear helping us to maintain equilibrium. The way this works, briefly, is that our inner ear contains crystals as well as fluid. When we change direction, the fluid pushes these crystals in different directions. The canals which hold the crystals are connected to the vestibular nerve, which sends the information about the position of the crystals to the brain. Our wonderful grey matter interprets the information sent to it, and immediately sends instructions to different parts of the body so they can move to help us maintain balance. Unfortunately, this is something that as soccer coaches, we cannot influence. Progress in balance is a series of developmental stages for young children. Those of us who are parents will know that, in most cases, our babies learned to sit up unsupported around the age of six months. Our midwives or paediatric nurses probably also advised us to give our babies 'tummy time', time laying on their fronts. This will have helped them to develop core strength which also aids the process towards becoming more agile. So, like soccer coaches with older children, as parents we influenced and sped up the process towards out baby being able to sit up, but we could not instil this until our little one was ready.

(There is another key point here. Whilst we are not in any way suggesting work outs in a local gym are in any way appropriate not only for six to ten year olds, but for any pre-fully pubescent children, lots of different activities help to develop core strength. When our players have good core strength, they become more agile. If we align that improved agility to strong ball skills, we have better soccer players. Which is a long way of saying that there is nothing wrong and much good to including elements in our training sessions which involve different types of movement with or without a ball.)

Back to our babies. At around a year they typically begin their cruising – that frightening time for parents which largely involves shifting anything breakable to a height our nearly-toddler cannot reach as they make their way around the room with remarkable speed, supported by the table, the sofa, the dog, or any other object which lends them a hand. Six months on, most babies are walking free, thus moving completely from the baby stage to the toddler one. It is not going to be too much after this that they join our soccer team. That we get young children able to run, to jump, to change direction, to move with a ball under control, to strike that ball from various positions and in various directions is truly remarkable, if we think about it. What we have are young people with remarkable agility, really, although of course that agility is going to get much better over the coming years.

Our job is to give as many opportunities for our players to further develop their core strength and balance in as many fun ways as possible.

If that is a very brief insight into balance, then coordination is a little more complex. Fundamentally, by coordination we mean an awareness – at the instinctive level – of where our muscles and limbs are, and what they are doing, during different activities. The process is called proprioception. So, for example, if we throw our heads to one side, keep our arms firmly down, ensure our non-kicking foot is well back from the ball and attempt to shoot as hard and far as possible, not only will our shot miscue, but most likely we will fall over too. As soccer coaches we know that our heads, arms and non-kicking foot are essential for shooting, as important as the foot that strikes the ball. A six year old starting out does not know that. If they do not instinctively position their body correctly, they will need to be taught how to do so.

Some young children will naturally position their limbs and muscles correctly to strike the ball. Chances are these are children who have already experienced a wide range of actions and movements – through play – which has already instilled in them a sense of coordination when faced with a new activity.

For those of us working towards the younger age covered by this book, most likely our players will generally already hold some of the coordination techniques required, but not all of them. For example, through playing chasing games at pre-school and in early years education, or simply running around the park with their parents, they will naturally use their arms for balance. Their heads though, may move in all sorts of directions.

The following drills are designed to help children develop agility and coordination. To be fair, however, the quickest way they will learn and ingrain these developmental stages is through their own play. But as coaches, we can also enhance the opportunities for this. If our sessions are friendly, fun and social, our players are likely to develop further friendships and buddies with which they will play. It is through that play that both their agility and their coordination will come on in leaps and bounds.

Soccer Drill: Obstacle Course

A warmup activity here. It takes a bit of setting up, so works best where coaches can prepare in advance, or while the group is taking another activity. Quite often training pitches are in public parks and include a play area. If it works for you, why not incorporate a couple of circuits into the session? Meet there, and then jog across to your training area?

However, an obstacle course is easily created simply from the equipment to which most clubs and coaches will have access. Really, we are just looking to create a trail which involves numerous activities, some with a ball, some without, so the example below is just that, an example. Albeit one which makes use of standard soccer drill equipment.

This seems a good point to address the question of whether to stretch or not to stretch. Neither I nor my team in writing this book are doctors, or medically qualified, so we can only offer an opinion based on our experience. That suggests that children aged six to eight do not need to stretch prior to starting a coaching session. At this age, they are naturally moving all the time, constantly running, dodging and doing all the things that a stretching session will address. So we would suggest it is not necessary. However, stretching becomes good practice for when the children are older and will benefit from proper stretching activities before warming up. Plus, of course, they will have seen their professional heroes going through their paces prior to matches on TV, so an activity such as an obstacle course can include some stretching activities. Less for the benefit it brings aged six, but more as a marker for the future.

Use With: Any age.

Objectives: Undertake a number of activities to improve agility.

Equipment: Whatever is to hand. To replicate this particular course cones, mannequins, balls, goals and a training ladder are required.

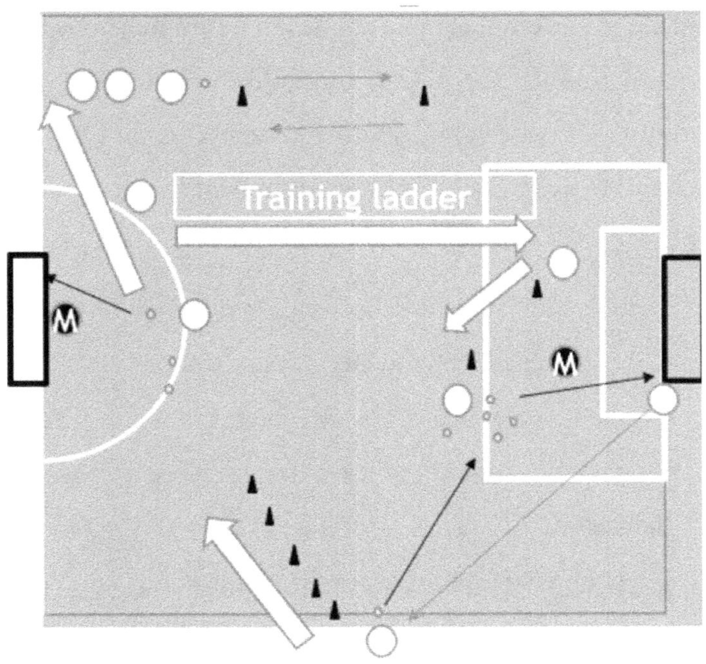

In the diagram above for ease of following, we have used a 'white dot' player at each of the aspects of the drill. This is meant to represent the same player working through the drill.

Operation of Drill: Run through the drill once, with the players following the coach as he or she demonstrates each aspect of the course. Then, move to the beginning and set the players off one at a time, with the next player going as soon as the first has completed the initial activity. Run through the course three times for each player. Below are the different aspects of the drill.

- Dribble runs – dribble between two cones, turn, and dribble back. One ball, two cones required.
- Quick step through a training ladder. Training ladder required. In some countries, this is called an agility ladder.
- High step between two cones. Cones required
- Shoot into a goal past a mannequin. Collect ball and dribble to side of pitch. Balls, goal and mannequin required. Keep a small number of balls at this element of the drill to ensure it does not slow down too much.
- Take a throw in, throwing the ball back to the shooting area just visited. (Same ball)
- Dodge course, through cones.

- Take a penalty. Maybe have a coach or mannequin here as a keeper, or just an empty goal. Equipment required – goal, balls, perhaps keeper/mannequin.
- Run backwards to beginning of course and join back of line.

Key Skills:

- Various activities to help develop agility.
- Shooting technique.
- Throw-in within the laws of the game.

Development:

- Add or remove elements of the course as required. For example, rather than dodging through cones, dribble a ball through the cones.

Soccer Drill: Changing Direction

Young children are often good at running in a straight line, but much less so at changing direction. This simple to set up drill helps them to learn to change direction quickly.

Use With: Any age, but the younger and less skilled the players are, the bigger the area in which they should work.

Objectives: Dribble with the ball under control, changing direction regularly.

Equipment: Grid, twenty metres by twenty metres. A penalty area, or with a smaller group, centre circle, works just as well. Balls, one between two.

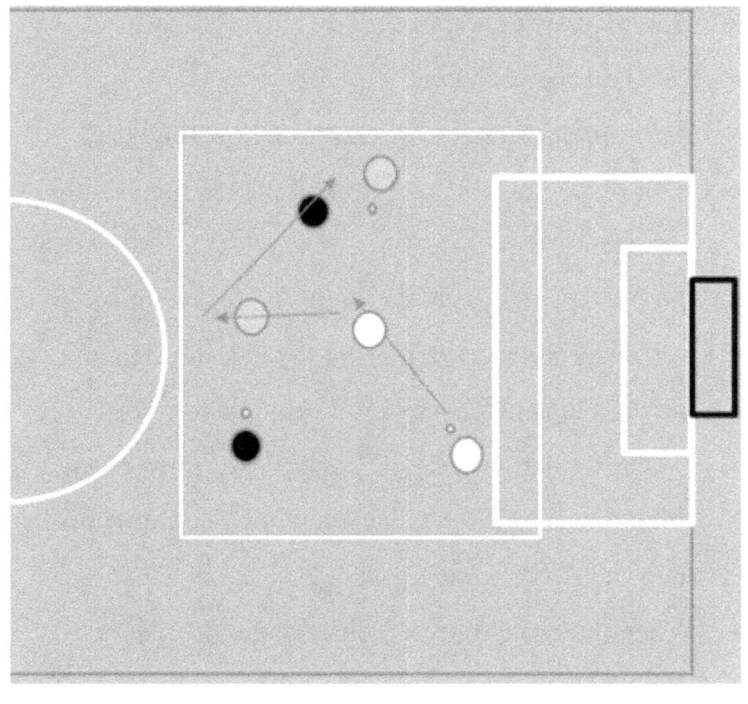

In the diagram above, we show only the movement of the player represented by the white dot. In reality, one player each in the black and white pair will also be dribbling, so there will be much more movement than a two-dimensional static diagram can represent.

Operation of Drill:

- Get the players to pair up.

- One ball between two.

- Pairs spread themselves within the playing grid.

- First player has the ball, second player stands still, legs apart.

- On the whistle, the player with the ball dribbles anywhere in the grid, putting the ball through any player's legs, dribbling round any player.

- Coach shouts 'CHANGE', and player must change direction as quickly as they can, then continue on their dribble.

- When the coach blows their whistle, the player dribbles back to their partner and they change roles.

Key Skills:

- Dribbling with the ball under close control.
- Changing direction on instruction.
- Passing with accuracy between the legs of another player.
- Coach encourages the following agility skills:
  - Move on toes to allow rapid changes of direction,
  - Move the ball only short distances…
    - Using the toes.
    - Using the instep to turn.
    - Using the outside of the foot.
    - (A lot of the players will find this difficult but will begin to get it in time.)
  - Use arms out for balance and stability.
  - Drop body weight on turn.
  - Kick off rear foot to accelerate away.

Development:

- As players become more skilled at this activity, reduce the playing area.

Soccer Drill: Narrow Spaces

A very simple drill which children enjoy because they can get a lot of success with it. With the very youngest and least experienced, do away with the goalkeepers to make it easier to achieve the reward of scoring a goal.

Use With: Younger players, under sixes etc, or those new to the game.

Objectives: Dribble in a straight line, then change direction while dribbling. Dribble at a speed which allows the ball to stay under control.

Equipment: Cones, balls, goals.

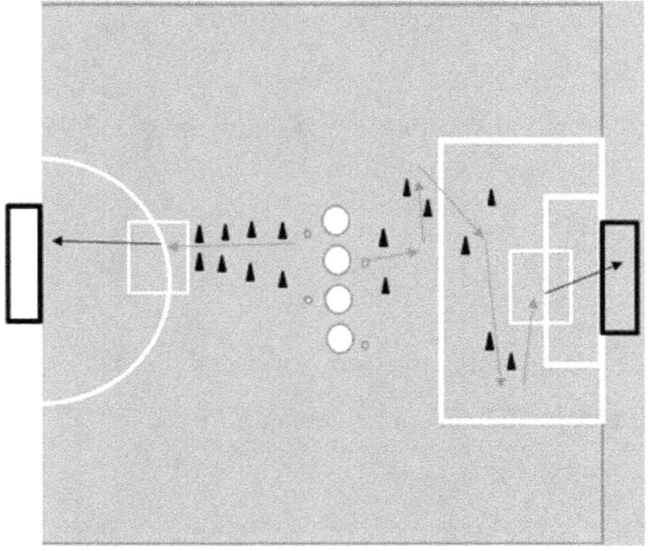

Operation of Drill:

- Set up pairs of cones getting increasingly close together.
- Set up two cones by each goal as a shooting zone.
- Players dribble between cones, then enter the shooting zone, and attempt to score either past the goalkeeper or into an empty net.

- First set of cones require dribbling under control in a straight line.

- Second set of cones require some changing of direction.

- Players move between one set of cones and the other.

Key Skills:

- Dribbling using the laces for a straight line.

- Learning that accuracy and control are initially more important than speed.

- Staying light on toes with arms out for balance.

- Shooting with laces.

Development:

- Once players have mastered the basic skill, narrow the dribbling zone.

- Add more turns. Introduce goalkeepers (if not already in play.)

Soccer Drill: Weaker Foot

We all know that the best players are two footed. Although the likelihood is that almost all players will be stronger on one side than the other, a two footed player is confident enough to control the ball, pass and shoot with both feet.

The earlier we can get a player to develop that confidence in their weaker side, the easier it becomes to turn them into two footed players.

Use With: Any age, but the younger the better

Objectives: Pass with weaker foot. Change direction quickly. Shoot with both feet.

Equipment: Cones, balls, goal, goalkeeper.

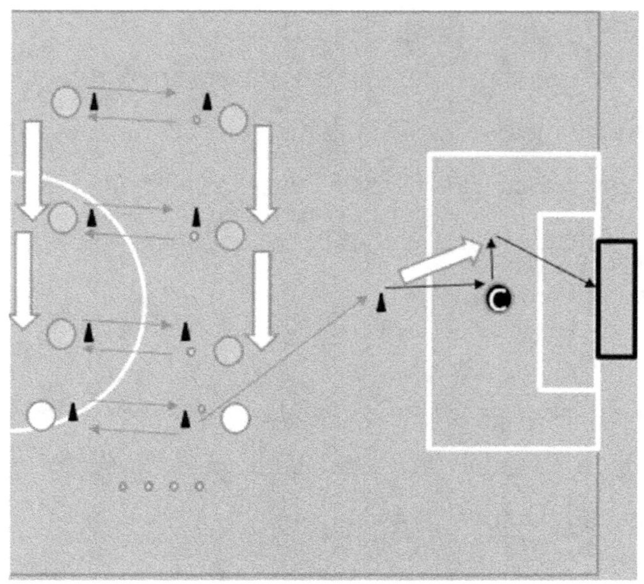

In the diagram, we show one full cycle of the drill, with the grey players moving down the line of cones each time the end set becomes available. After shooting, as explained below, the players move back to the beginning of the pairs of cones.

Operation of Drill: This is a very simple drill, commonly used, but is beneficial for its simplicity. Coaches should be aware of being especially encouraging as success may be harder to come by than with other drills, and young players thrive on success. (In fact, all players thrive on success, whatever their age!)

The passing drill included here is to ensure that players are kept busy so the coach can concentrate on advising on technique, rather than keeping players focussed. Managing behaviour detracts from coaching time, and the best way not to have to manage behaviour is to keep our players busy. Where a second coach is available, they should supervise this passing element of the drill.

- Set up pairs of cones five metres apart. These are for players to practice passing to each other firstly with their weaker foot.
    - Where a second coach is available to oversee this element, stress the importance of duplicating the actions for passing with their stronger foot.

- As each pair of cones at the front become clear, players dribble and move to the next set of cones.
  - Now they swap to pass with their other foot. And so on until it becomes their turn to do the main drill.
- In the main drill the player dribbles to the isolated cone on the right, then passes with their weaker foot into the coach. (Note: it is important to use a coach rather than another player here within the six to ten age range. The drill is certainly useful to older players and can be carried out with any age. As players become older the role of the feeder can be taken by a player, but here use the coach as the players are very young, and the drill does not work if the feed is poor.)
- The player continues to run on to the ball.
- The coach passes to either side. Note – not always to the player's weaker foot, sometimes to the stronger. (The use of the stronger foot in both the shooting and the passing elements of the drill are to

help players keep technique in the forefront of their thinking.)

- The player takes no more than two touches then shoots, using the laces to generate pace.
- There are a collection of spare balls by the last pair of cones so the partner can collect one before dribbling to the cone and passing to the coach.
- Player collects the ball, then heads back to the passing cones, and waits for a partner to begin the passing drill again.

Key Skills:

- Replicating the acts of passing and shooting, using the weaker rather than stronger foot.
- Shooting:
  - Arms for balance.
  - Run onto the ball for the shot.
  - Non-kicking foot planted to the side and very slightly behind the ball.

- o Smooth swing with the kicking foot, striking the
  ball with the laces.
  - o Smooth follow through.
- Passing:
  - o Arms for balance.
  - o Stay on toes to allow rapid change of direction to
    get into position.
  - o Move to get into position to control the ball with
    instep.
  - o Knock the ball fifteen centimetres to the side and
    forward (forty five degrees, but players of this
    age are unlikely to understand this concept).
  - o Move into position to get head over the ball.
  - o Non kicking foot planted to side of ball.
  - o Strike with instep, chest facing the direction of
    travel of the ball.
  - o Strike smoothly and follow through.

Development:

- If no goalkeeper, add one.

- This is a difficult skill, so it will take time to master. Where players do begin to become competent with their weaker foot, try introducing some low level defensive elements, such as a cone to dribble past, or a mannequin.

Soccer Drill: Handball

There is no question that children aged six to ten are still mastering dexterity, coordination and agility. There is equally no doubt that they are more competent with their hands than feet, and more dexterous at larger movement than fine movements. Therefore we can help them develop their whole body agility by playing games which either do not use a ball or involve catching and throwing rather than kicking.

The following drill encourages fast thinking and anticipatory movement, so builds skills required in soccer, but without that pesky nuisance of having to control and kick a ball.

Use With: Any age, but the drill is designed to use with the youngest and least experienced children in the range.

Objectives: Score a 'goal' by catching and throwing the ball. Move to find space.

Equipment: 30 x 20m grid. 'Goal' on opposite ends. Balls. Bibs.

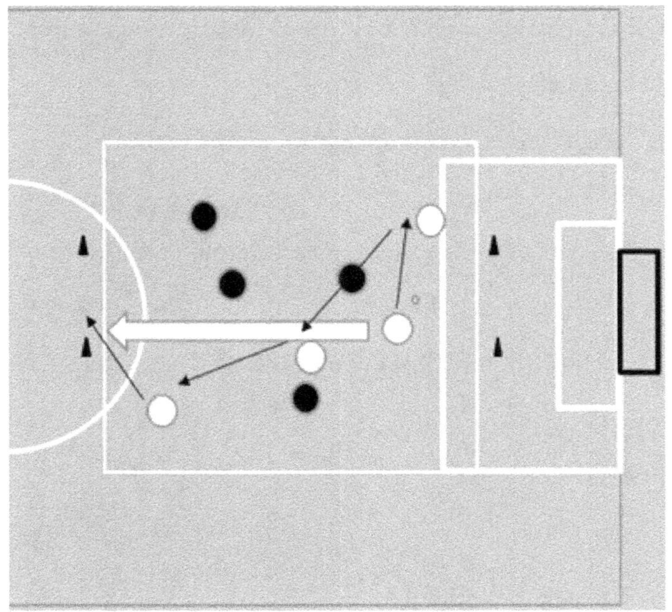

Operation of Drill: The game can be played with up to eight versus eight, just make the pitch bigger in this situation. However, it works best with four versus four, mostly because the smaller the sides the more touches player receive.

- The ball is passed with throws between teammates.
- No running with the ball.

- One bounce maximum on passes, or possession changes.

- No tackling, but interceptions allowed.

- A 'goal' is scored when the ball is caught by the 'keeper' standing between the goal cones.

- Game 'kicks off' with possession to the goalkeeper of the side who have just conceded.

Key Skills:

- Movement to find space.

- Body position right to receive ball.

- Agile thinking for quick passing and movement to receive ball.

Development:

- Allow goalkeepers to join the pitch, encouraging the thinking that goalkeepers have a role beyond just saving the ball.
- Allow any player to become the goalkeeper by standing on the line between posts. (Advisory note: only allow one player to do this at any one time – in order to avoid disagreements over who is going to catch the 'shot'!)

Agility and coordination, rather like spatial awareness, develop in time. They are traits which develop through practice. A good coach can aid this by playing lots of short, active, games. But the challenge we face as coaches is that practice is by its nature repetitive and thus can become boring. But we can counter this by using two simple sounding but in practice slightly harder techniques.

The first of these is praise. Children love praise, they thrive on it. So provide it all the time, and not just with words, but with body language and tone of voice too. Secondly, variety. Decide on the core trait or skill to be developed and try to provide as many varied activities as possible to promote this. Although, we do advise to keep it simple. A good investment for the coach of younger players is a set of rugby tag belts. These are belts with two removable tags strips velcroid on either side of the hips. They allow for lots of tag type games, such as bulldog and 'It' to be played safely as there is no body contact. These games encourage dodging, changes of body position and changes in speed which help children develop their coordination and agility naturally, in a safe and fun environment.

LEVEL 2 –PLAYING WITH OTHERS

Developing Teamwork – Passing Drills

Whilst the first two drill-based chapters have had as their focus speeding the acquisition of developmental traits, those essential in good soccer players, they have nevertheless not had the acquisition of soccer specific skills at their heart. Over the next three chapters we will begin to look at skills which are connected directly with the playing of our sport. However, in doing so, we pay heed to the point made in the opening chapter and link these skills directly to the personal and emotional developmental stage our players will hold. Therefore, these skills are individual ones, rather than tactical, strategic or connected to formations.

If our motivation is winning leagues with Under Sixes, then we have no real need of tactics or formations. As we said earlier, just put the longest kicker at the back, and the fastest runner up front, and victory will be gained over teams run by coaches who take a longer term view. For a while, at least. And two of your players will develop. Even if the remainder lose interest. As long as, of course, by the time they reach the age of eleven or twelve, they are still the biggest and quickest, and other players properly coached have not left them behind.

We are being facetious, of course, although the point still holds. It is absolutely right, and proper and reasonable that as coaches we love soccer. With that comes the fact that soccer is a competitive game, so it follows that the likelihood is that we are by our nature competitive people, at least in the sporting arena. Holding back that competitive instinct while working with young children will be one of the (many) challenging elements of coaching six- to ten-year-olds. But it cannot be stated often enough that if we do not hold it back, our coaching skills are compromised, as will be the progress of our players.

With this blunt point in mind, the following three chapters will focus on those individual skills of passing (in this chapter), dribbling and shooting.

Of the three, teaching our players to pass the ball is perhaps the most challenging and that is because of the developmental stage through which our players are progressing. Particularly the youngest ones in the age group. As explained earlier, some will still be quite firmly entrenched in an egocentric stage of their development. So, when we see them running into a cul de sac, ball bobbling in front of them, it is not that they do not want to pass, but very simply their perspective on the game is very much based around their own involvement in it. If they have the ball, that must be good. If they give it to a teammate, make a pass, then their involvement is, in their eyes, reduced, so the thought that passing might be a good thing to do never occurs to them.

Of course, that can be frustrating for us as coaches, who are able to see a bigger picture. Especially so for parent watchers, who (in the occasional case) drift back to their own egocentric period, re-living it through their own child, and thus demand the ball be passed to little Jimmy or show their anxiety that Annie is not in possession.

Nevertheless, for most children even of six, this stage of development is close to ending, or has ended already and so it is definitely worth persisting with helping our players to improve their passing. Again, though, in the context of a fun and busy drill.

Soccer Drill: Technique for Striking the ball.

There are a number of essential elements when teaching young children techniques. It is human nature to want to be as clear as possible, and our desire to do our best for our young players is often such that we lose sight of the fact that we are working with very small children indeed. Their concentration span is typically short, and their perception of what we want is often sufficiently far from our intentions that we cannot quite understand what they are doing when we release them to put our words into practice. In fact, we should treat it as a victory if some of the players produce something even vaguely resembling what we hope for.

So, we find these tips are handy ones to follow.

- Keep explanations short.
- Show rather than say; get players to do rather than watch.
- Break elements down into very short and simple parts.
- Design activities which give opportunity for reward and success.

We need one to one time with each player to ensure technique is grasped as quickly as possible. This presents the challenge of what to do with the other players during this moment of attention. This drill attempts to satisfy this problem. The most value, though, comes from the one-to-one element of the drill.

Use With: Beginners. Depending on how the players progress, it may be best to break the drill with a different activity to ensure players do not become bored.

Objectives: Establish the techniques of head and body position, striking with the instep and position of the non-kicking foot.

Equipment: Three goals, each with a couple of balls. Cones. Coach, or coaches (the more the better). Check list – players name and the three objectives, so as each is successfully completed it is ticked off and the coach can focus on the next skill.

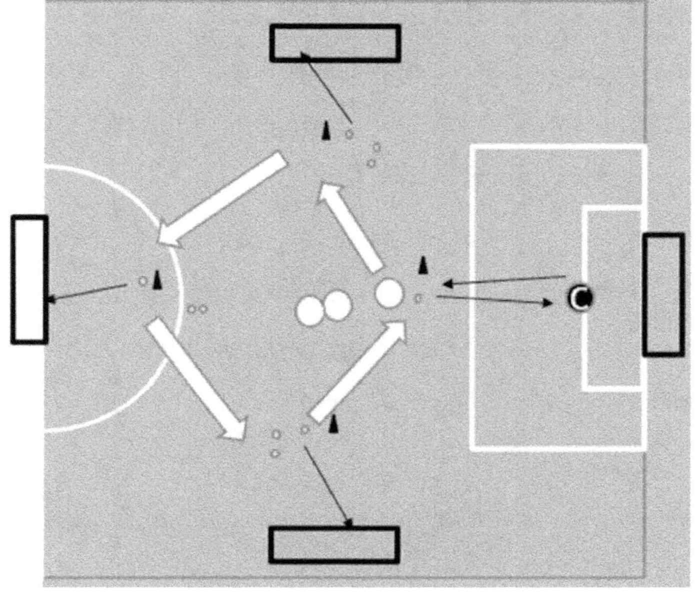

Operation of Drill:

The Less Important bit.

- After their one-to-one pass tuition with the coach (key element of the drill), the player runs to each of the goals.
- Player collects a ball, places it by the cone, and scores into the empty net with a pass.

- When it is their turn for the one-to-one passing attempt, they tell the coach how many they score. (This is for the reward element, and to help keep the players focussed - it has no significance for the objectives of the drill.)

The More Important bit. Pass practice with coach.

- Player passes the ball to the coach. Key here is to face coach when passing, ensuring body and head are pointing towards the coach.
- Coach gives feedback on this technique only.
- After one or two passes, play moves to the three goal scoring element of the drill, then joins the line for their next one to one pass.
- Once completed successfully twice in a row, the coach moves on to guiding player in second technique.
- Coach demonstrates how to pass with instep, keeping body in line and having a smooth follow through.

- Player replicates.

- Repeat above.

- Coach demonstrates placement of non-kicking foot, to the side of the ball.

- Repeat as above.

With young, inexperienced players the technique will need to be emphasised regularly to ensure it becomes ingrained in the skills the players are developing.

Key Skills:

- Facing the player to receive the pass.
- Striking with the instep.
- Smooth follow through.
- Non-kicking foot planted firmly to the side and fractionally behind the ball.

Development:

- Once these skills are mastered the coach can move onto to other forms of passing, such as with the outside of the foot.

Soccer Drill: Passing with the Outside of the foot.

A simple drill, with a competitive element for fun, which aims to help players naturally play the ball with the outside of their foot. Of course, this is quite a tough skill, but by introducing it early and with the understanding that it may take time to acquire, we are establishing a wider range of passing among our players. There is only good in this, provided our expectations are high and match the experience and development of our players.

Use With: All ages, although with younger players we are mostly aiming to make the movement feel natural.

Objectives: Make four passes with the outside of the foot around a grid before a teammate can run the complete perimeter of the grid.

Equipment: Cones to make a grid. Ball.

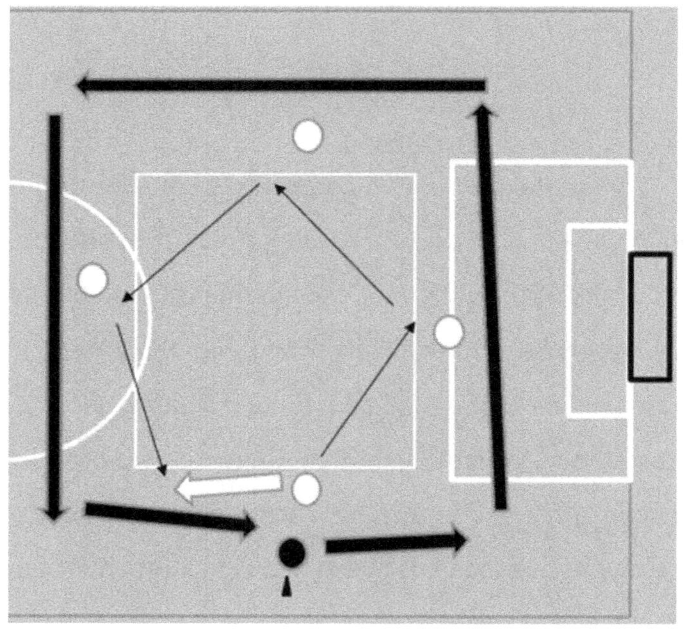

Operation of Drill:

- Divide the players into groups of five.

- One player on each side of the approximately eight by eight metre grid.

- Fifth player is the 'runner'. They stand by a cone (or they can start at a corner) which marks the start and finish of their running route around the grid.

- The ball begins with the player nearest to the 'runner'.

- The four players must pass the ball across the grid in turn using the outside of the foot. They can use any part of the body, including their hands, to control the ball as it is passed to them.

- They 'runner' must run outside the grid.

- The four players aim to get the ball back to the first passer before the runner gets to the corner from which they set off. Use the arrows in the grid above to see directions of passes.

- Switch the runner after each circuit.

- Whilst this is a self and peer taught exercise, the coach should circulate, offering tips and guidance as groups complete a circuit.

Key Skills:

- Striking with the outside of the foot.
- Self-learning. The player will begin to feel what seems natural to them.
- Peer learning. As the players will want to beat the 'runner', they will share their own tips.
- Self-learning (technically called metacognitive learning – this is where a person identifies what they need to know and seeks sources of guidance in order to satisfy that need) is generally understood to be the highest and therefore most effective form of learning. Developing the ability to do this while young will not only help players' soccer playing development, but their more general learning as well.
- Peer learning is also a very effective way to acquire skills and techniques.

- (Indeed, the coach as teacher is, sadly for us, one of the least effective ways of enabling young people to acquire skills – or indeed knowledge. The very best coaches – and teachers – use their experience and knowledge to facilitate learning for their charges, rather than impart their knowledge. Consider the very best professional coaches – Pep Guardiola, Jurgen Klopp, Arsene Wenger, Brian Clough to name just four who have advanced the game in England, for example – and their skills are even more in man management – facilitating learning – than in their encyclopaedic knowledge of the game.

Development:

- As players become more proficient, allow them to control the ball only with their feet, weighting their touch so they can immediately pass on.

Soccer Drill: Receiving the Pass on the Half Turn

This may seem like a complex skill to introduce to young children, and true, it is a difficult technique to acquire. But there is no reason not to start young. As with the previous, a good coach keeps the elements simple, and breaks them down into manageable chunks.

Use With: Any age.

Objectives: Control the pass with the body correctly positioned on the half-turn.

Equipment: Balls, mannequins (these are not strictly necessary, and could be replaced with cones.)

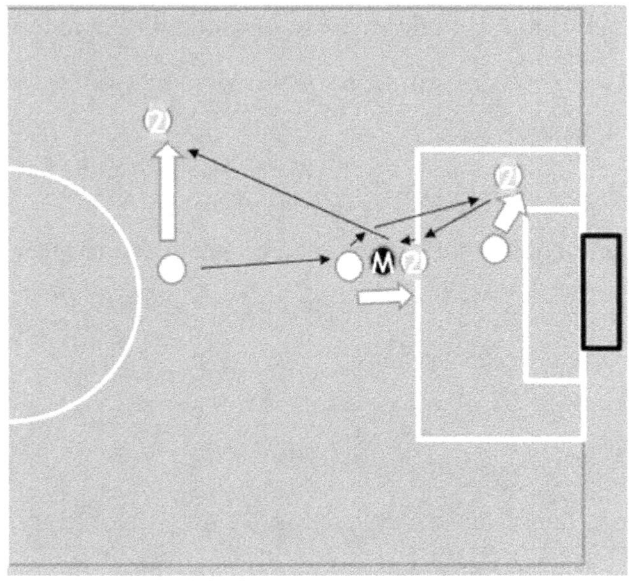

In the diagram above, the plain white dots show the initial positions of the receiver and the two passers, the 'Number 2' dots show the same players, but in their positions for subsequent passes.

Operation of Drill:

- Divide players into groups of three.
- One ball and one mannequin per group.

- The group is made up of two passers and a receiver.
- Receiver stands in front of the mannequin.
- Pass into the receiver.
- Receiver reaches behind them to touch the mannequin. Their other arm comes forwards to keep balance as they take a step towards the ball.
  - So, reach behind.
  - Other arm forwards.
  - Step towards the ball.
  - These movements naturally turns their body into the half turn position.
- We can create a name for the movement. For example, helicopter, or aeroplane.
- Receiver allows the ball to strike their front foot. (Later we can introduce inside and outside of foot control, to keep control of the turn. For now, this may be a step too far.)
- Whichever way the ball deflects, player turns, and passes to the third player in their group (the receiver who has not yet been given a pass.

- Receiver moves to the other side of the mannequin for the drill to continue.
- After a few passes, swap the receiver.

Key Skills:

- Body position.
- Weight of pass from feeders to allow the ball to be controlled, and also deflect a little off the foot.

Development:

- As body position is mastered, the coach can tell players to experiment with controlling the ball with the inside or outside of their foot.

Soccer Drill: Passing Rondo

This is a match practice, offense versus defense, type game where one side is weighted with more players.

There is only one physical goal here as such, but points are scored through accurate passing.

Use With: Any age. Young children have an acute sense of fairness, and it may be necessary to explain that this is not an even game, and one side has the advantage. Make it clear that this is because we are all one team, and the drill will help us to become better players. It does not matter if one side scores more goals the other.

Objectives: Pass to make best use of the overload of players.

Equipment: One goal, ball, small pitch, cones to mark 'passing line'.

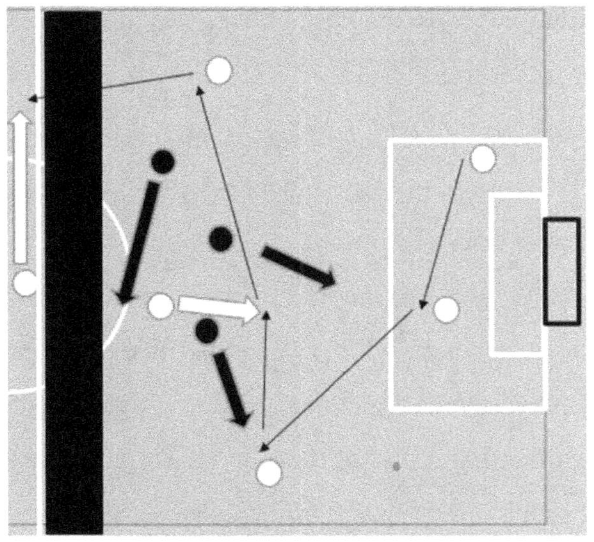

Operation of Drill:

- Pitch has proper goal at one end. No goalkeeper. This is the goal into which the team of three can score points.

- For the other end, the 'goal' is the goal line (Marked on the diagram by the white line stretching across the pitch). Five metres in front of the goal line is the 'no entry zone.' (This is marked by the solid black rectangle on the diagram above.) No attacking player may enter this.

- Two teams. One of six players, one of three.
- In the team of six, one player is positioned behind the goal line.
- Points or goals are scored by the team of six through passing accurately through to the 'no entry zone' for the player behind the line to control with their feet or any other legal part of their body. They must control the ball behind the line and close to their feet.
- The team of three score by passing into the empty net at the other end.

Key Skills:

- Passing quickly and accurately to create space. Players will learn that dribbling allows the defence to get in position to stop an attack, whereas passing creates space for a point scoring opportunity.
- Communication to aid quick passing.
- Finding space to receive a pass.

- (Both teams will learn about speed on transition. This is a strategy as much as a skill, so should not be explicitly worked on, better to let it emerge naturally as players become familiar with the drill.)

Development:

- Limit touches to prevent dribbling.

Soccer Drill: Limited Touch League

With young children, space is important if they are to limit their touches on the ball. The league can be played over a number of weeks, or an entire session can be given over to it. If this is possible, then progress will be quicker, but this will require enough space to mark out several pitches.

Use With: Any age. Very inexperienced players will find this quite difficult.

Objectives: Pass accurately. Move to find space. Communicate.

Equipment: Many cones to mark out small pitches. Different coloured cones to make small goals. Bibs.

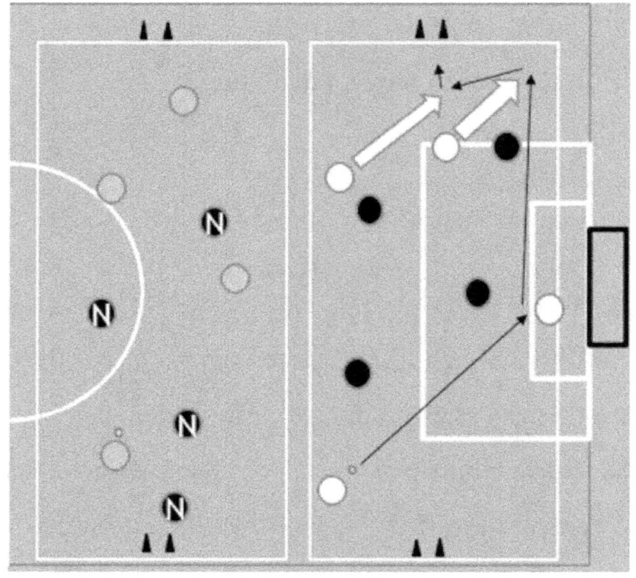

Operation of Drill:

- Divide group into teams of three, or at the most four.

- Mark out and number pitches (for ease of organisation). It should be possible to make four pitches (two in each half) on a normal six a side pitch.
- Make a narrow goal using different coloured cones at each end of each pitch.
- Set a limit of touches. Talented under eights should manage three or even two touch games. Inexperienced sixes might need four touches.
- Possession switches if too many touches without a pass are made.
- No goalkeepers.
- Short games. Five minutes is a good length. This comfortably allows for nine games in a one hour session, the length of games can be adapted.
- Time does need to be allowed for organising change of pitches and allocating games. However, eight teams (which is a lot, as it involves twenty four players) involves only seven rounds of matches and four pitches.

- Coach should have prepared a results grid and a fixture list in advance to allow smooth flow of the tournament.
- It is advantageous to have a referee for each game, but this is not essential. One coach can oversee the tournament.

Key Skills:

- Working as a team.
- Developing touch to set in position for a pass.
- Movement to find space.
- Communication to make passing easier.
- Passing technique to improve accuracy of passing.

Development:

- If time, have play offs – first in the league v second etc.
- Higher team can start with a 'penalty' into the empty goal in recognition of their higher placing.

- Introduce home and away fixtures, home team starting with the penalty. (This involves most probably a number of weeks for the competition, and there is then the risk that players may be absent making the organisation of the tournament difficult.)
- Get other clubs involved, and host a limited touch tournament…

If scoring goals is the ultimate aim in soccer, then it is through passing that opportunities for goal scoring are created. Children of six or seven are still quite egocentric, in that their perception of the world around them is taken from the context of their own position in the world. Therefore, the value of passing is something that players will need to acquire, as much as the skills and techniques required to make those passes. Again, as coaches we should expect that even though we might hold a brilliant session, focussed on passing, which delivers excellent results, by Saturday's game we might see very little evidence of the week's practice. Acquiring skills happens quite quickly with young children, getting them sufficiently ingrained that they become automatic is a much longer process. That's something a little beyond our control as coaches. Unfortunately. It is a part of a child's natural development, and even the best sixty minutes once a week is going to have little impact on two million years of evolution! Accept that, and we are on our way to becoming the best under ten coach that we can be.

A Short message from the Author:

Hey, are you enjoying the book? I'd love to hear your thoughts!

Many readers do not know how hard reviews are to come by, and how much they help an author.

I would be incredibly thankful if you could take just 60 seconds to write a brief review on Amazon, even if it's just a few sentences!

Your review will genuinely make a difference for me and help gain exposure for my work.

LEVEL 3 – GETTING COMFORTABLE WITH THE BALL

Dribbling Drills

If one of the main challenges of getting young children to pass the ball is that it involves seeing beyond themselves, something developmentally difficult for kids of this age, then the opposite is true of dribbling. Our challenge is most likely to be stopping them from dribbling all the time. We can therefore use that developmental egocentricity to our advantage. Dribbling is what young children like to do, so let's take the opportunity to teach them to do it right.

Soccer Drill: Dribbling at Speed

Children love to run, so this drill takes advantage of this. As are all the best practices for youngsters starting out on their soccer careers, simplicity is the key. No complex instructions, only one thing to remember yet important repetition helps to ingrain the skill.

Use With: Any age. Every soccer player needs, at times, to run with the ball.

Objectives: Dribble using the laces without leaving a defined track.

Equipment: Cones to create tracks. Balls.

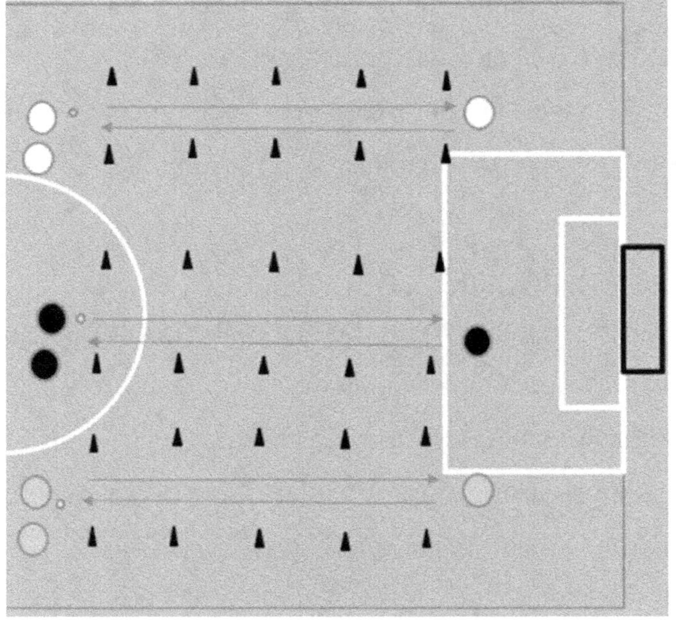

Operation of Drill:

- Set up a number of tracks about two metres wide.

- Divide players up into groups of at least three.

- Place each group at either end of a track. The front player at one of the ends starts with that group's ball. This player must have at least one other teammate at their end. It does not matter how many are facing him or her, provided there is at least one player there behind them.

- Player dribbles slowly to the opposite end, trying to keep the ball within the tracks by using their laces.

- As competence increases, players are encouraged to go faster.

- If ball leaves the track, the player brings it back and continues on their dribble. Highlight the importance of not getting in the way of other players if doing this.

- Lots of encouragement from the coach helps to maintain enthusiasm.

Key Skills:

- Dribbling using the laces to propel the ball.
- Get players to run on their toes.
- Arms out for balance.
- Try to get players to look up at the player they are running towards.

Development:

- Narrow the track as competence improves.

Soccer Drill: Gateways

This is a handy drill, also useful as a warmup, because it keeps every player involved at all times. Again, simplicity is the key. A variation of the drill (see 'development') helps young children understand that they are part of a team, so when somebody makes a mistake, all players pay a penalty. But they work together rather than apportion blame.

Use With: Ages six to eight, but the drill works with players a little younger and older.

Objectives: Dribble through the gates without letting your ball hit another ball or player.

Equipment: Cones for grid. Cones to mark out gates. Enough balls for one each. (Four more cones and bibs for development option.)

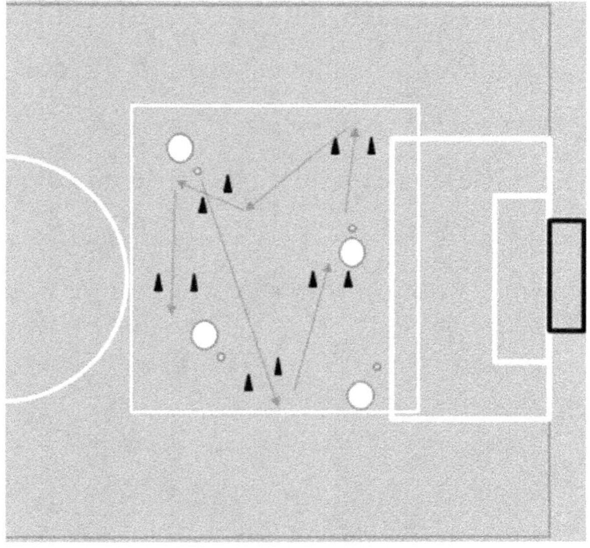

Operation of Drill:

- Set up a reasonably large grid, say thirty metres by thirty metres, larger or smaller depending on numbers.
- Place a number of two metre wide gates inside the grid.
- Players dribble through the gates.
- They can travel through the gates in any direction and in any order.
- They cannot pass through the same gate without visiting at least two more in between. (This rule might only need specifying if a player simply dribbles back and forth through the same gate, which is unlikely.)
- Try to avoid contact with another player or their ball.

Key Skills:

- Dribbling under close control.
- Keeping head up to make sure collisions are avoided.

- Changing direction while dribbling.

Development:

- Place a cone ten metres outside each line of the grid.
- Divide the players into four teams.
- Whenever two players collide, every member of that team (or teams) must leave their ball, run to the nearest outside cone and do ten star jumps before returning.
- Emphasise fun not competition to avoid blame.

Soccer Drill: Cross the Wall Game

A fun game which helps children to improve their dribbling skills without knowing it. Basically, a variation on tag or bulldog, but with less danger!

Use With: Any age up to about Under 12s. Suitable for the full age range covered by this book.

Objectives: Dribble with the ball under control. Avoid being tackled as players cross the wall.

Equipment: Balls. Cones of two colours.

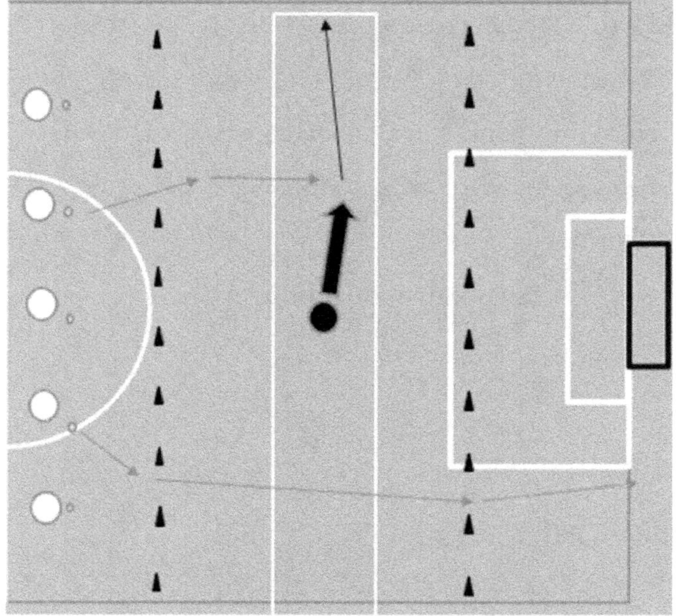

In the diagram above, the white box represents 'the wall'.

Operation of Drill:

- Create the playing area:
  - Use lines on pitch (e.g. halfway line and penalty area line) as starting and finishing points.
  - Ten metres from each place a line of cones. This marks the 'Danger Area'.
  - Halfway between the start and finish place two lines of different coloured cones ten metres apart. This is 'The Wall' and is the white box in the center.
- Choose one player to be the guard.
  - The guard can tackle anybody crossing the wall. No slide tackles allowed for safety reasons.
  - The guard can kick away any loose balls in the danger area, for example where a player (commando) has lost control of the ball or is running with the ball too far in advance of them to keep close control. They cannot tackle in the danger area.

- Commandos (the remaining players) run with the ball to the danger area, then dribble with close control through the danger area, wall and other danger area. Then run with the ball to the end line.
  - If a commando is tackled or loses control of the ball and it is kicked away, they become guards on the next run of the game.
  - If a commando is fouled then they receive a free pass through the wall and danger areas.

Key Skills:

- Dribbling using the laces to propel the ball.
- Dribbling with close control.
- Teamwork – when there are more guards, they develop strategy to make more tackles.

Development:

- Add gates to pass through to add additional pressure on the commandos.

Soccer Drill: One v One Killer Game

A drill to use on a pleasant, warm day. It is a drill which presents the opportunity for lots of enthusiastic cheering, although we advise playing the game with a careful eye towards over competitiveness or blame.

Use With: Any age up to under fourteens, so ideal with the age range covered by this book.

Objectives: Use dribbling and shooting skills to score goals in a one versus one game.

Equipment: Cones, balls, four small goals, bibs.

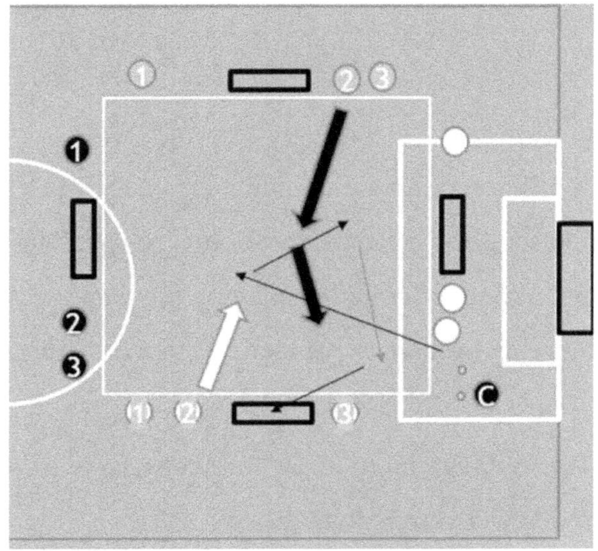

The game above shows just one of the two games in play. This is for ease of clarity in the diagram.

Operation of Drill:

- Create the playing area. Simple grid, with a small goal placed in the middle of each outer line.
- Divide the players into four teams.
- Give each player a bib and a number. For example, Red One, Blue Two.

- Each team is positioned on one line of the grid. The goal on that line is their goal, the one into which they must score.

- The coach kicks a ball into the grid and calls out one player from two of the teams. They can be any two of the teams. For example, Red One versus Green Three. It does not matter if these teams have goals opposite or at right angle to each other, a one versus one match ensues.

- The coach immediately kicks a second ball into the grid and starts a game between two players from the other teams.

- When a goal is scored, that game is over, but the other continues until a goal is scored.

- If a ball leaves the grid, the game is a draw.

- If the two balls hit each other, or players from *different matches* make contact, both games are a draw. (The exception is if a player deliberately makes contact with a player from another game in order to prevent losing their own game. At the age with which we are working such cynicism is unlikely.)

- If using the game with older children, it is worth keeping a tally of points. But with up to under tens, it is probably better to take each match as a self-contained unit, in order to prevent loss of motivation for the team who come in last.

Key Skills:

- Dribbling under close control.
- Skills to beat an opponent.
- Accurate shooting.
- Tackling.
- Spatial awareness of other balls and players.

Development:

- With more able players, make the pitch smaller.

Soccer Drill: Turning

We began this chapter with a specific skill – running with the ball – and will end it with another one. Turning. Watch young children and we will see this is something they often find very difficult, because their spatial awareness is at such an early stage of development. However, we have placed this drill within the context of a game.

Use With: The drill works well from about age five to age ten. It is ideal with under sevens and under eights.

Objectives: Dribble with the ball under close control, turning to avoid capture.

Equipment: Cones, balls.

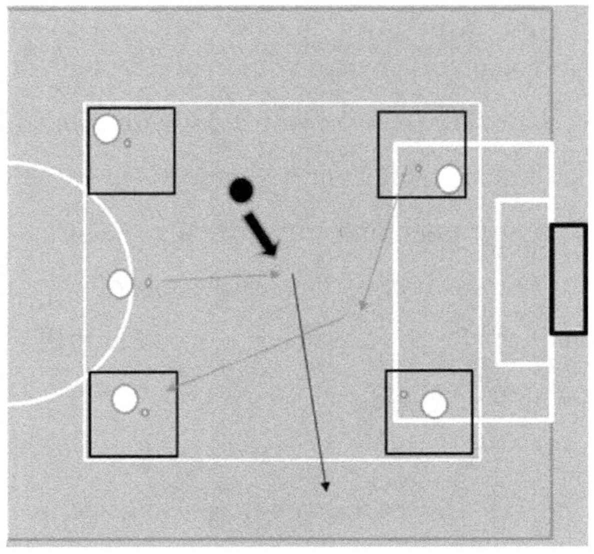

Operation of Drill:

- Create the playing area. Large thirty times thirty metre grid. In each corner of the grid is a small, five by five metre box. The four small boxes are islands. The remaining playing area is ocean.

- Divide the players more or less equally between the islands. These are the 'swimmers'. Choose one player to be the 'Great White Shark'. They do not have a ball.

- On the whistle, swimmers enter the ocean and must dribble to another island. If they are tackled, their ball leaves the grid or hits the ball of another player, they kick their ball outside the 'ocean' and become fellow Great White Sharks. (Coaches could have a list of killer fish – Barracuda, Tiger Shark, Hammerhead, Grouper, Giant Squid, Lionfish, Sting Ray, Man of War, Box Jelly Fish etc to name players when they become fish. Young children will enjoy that.)

- Note: it is worth running through the game without balls, with swimmers tagged rather than tackled the first time it is played. Then, when players understand the concept, introduce balls.

Key Skills:

- Dribbling under close control
- Turning.

Development:

- Introduce a shallow water channel (box in the middle) which swimmers must dribble through but fish cannot enter. This will ensure players get more practice as turning as their dribbling journey will be longer.

So much in soccer brings a thrill to the player, lifts a crowd, brings a smile. A great pass, threaded through a crowded midfield, a brilliant save, a bone crunching but legal tackle. Probably the second biggest thrill comes from watching a player weave past an opponent, beating them with a piece of skill, bursting into the space that trick creates. If that is the second biggest thrill in soccer, then there can be no doubt that the biggest cheer comes when a goal is scored. And in order to make the net bulge, it is necessary to take a shot. A thought which segues neatly into the next chapter.

Shooting Drills

Young children take lessons on board quickly. It might not always seem so, when we are trying to teach them a new skill or technique, but really their learning capacity is huge. Probably bigger than it will ever be in the future. But with that capacity comes a downside. If we teach a child to do something incorrectly, then the lesson is very hard to change. Not every shot in soccer leads to a goal, not every shot is saved brilliantly by a goalkeeper. Not every shot whistles just past the post. Sometimes, quite often in fact, that shot is closer to the corner flag than the goal, or flies over the bar as high as an aircraft passing over red lit cranes in a city. Or maybe it does bring a save from the keeper, but we can see that a pass would much more likely have resulted in a goal.

Our immediate instinct then is to point this out. Very quickly, with young children, the lesson they will take is that shooting is wrong. It leads to criticism, to a harsh word, or a disapproving facial expression, or groans from teammates. Once that lesson is ingrained, it will be very hard to lift our players' confidence when it comes to shooting, and the most thrilling aspect of playing soccer - scoring a goal – is denied to them.

So, as hard it may often be, it is vital to encourage shooting, to reward even poor shots (a **praise sandwich** can also be effective with young children; plenty of praise around a little constructive criticism – something like, 'Unlucky, great effort. Did you see Julie in the centre? If that had gone in, it would have been goal of the season. A worldie.') As children get older, like adults, they will start to ignore the surrounding praise and concentrate on the critical element, so the sandwich ceases to be effective, but six, seven, eight year olds, and for a few years to come, take the comment at face value, and will be encouraged.

When we learn we have to fail as part of the process. After all, if every time we shot, we scored, there would be no point in learning to shoot. The good coach embraces that failure, makes it a part of the learning process and develops confidence by focussing on the good. Our players will soon pick up on this, and they too will encourage shooting and reward attempts. Conversely, of course, they will also pick up on a coach's disapproving silence, or criticism, or facial expressions. They too will then reflect this by criticising the child who has taken the shot, lowering their confidence.

Soccer Drill: Pass and Shoot

This is a very good drill which is particularly handy for the coach because it involves players being active almost all of the time. It also helps to develop concentration and listening skills – very important in young children.

Use With: Under sixes to under eights. If using with older age groups make the pitch bigger and the goals smaller.

Objectives: Pass accurately, dribble effectively, listen carefully and shoot precisely. Quite a lot of objectives there for young children to take on board. Whilst all are essential in the drill, the most important on this occasion is the shooting element, although the opportunity for this will not emerge if the players fail to achieve the other objectives.

Equipment: Grid twenty metres by twenty metres, with a halfway line and a goal at one end. Balls.

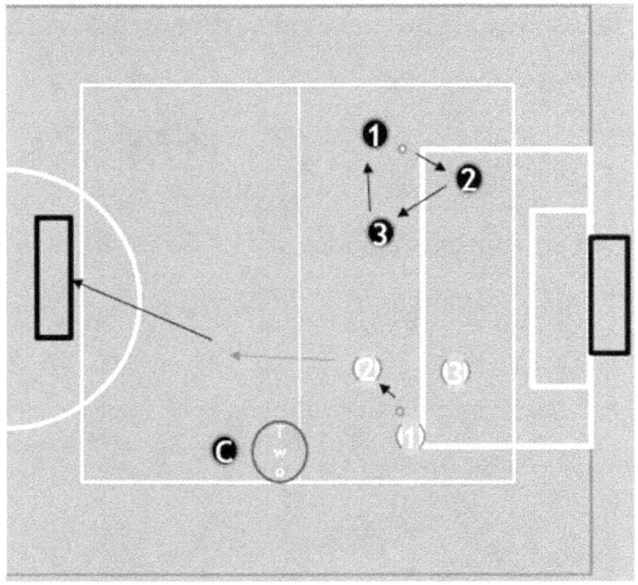

In the diagram, for ease of explanation and clarity, the numbered black team demonstrates what each team are doing prior to the coach calling 'Two', the numbered white team shows what happens after the coach's call.

Operation of Drill:

- Divide the players into groups of three. The drill as described is set up for two to four groups of three players each. If there are more, simply make the half without the goal larger.

- Number the players One, Two and Three. (Or give them each fun names, such as players from their local or national team, or greats – Pele, Maradona, Cruyff, for example).
- Each group has a ball.
- They begin in the half of the pitch without the goal and pass to each other.
- The coach calls a number.
- The player in possession in each group must immediately pass to that player.
- The player dribbles into other half, trying to keep the ball under good control.
- They open up for a shot and shoot into the goal.
- The ball is collected and the drill continues.

Key Skills:

- Getting into a position to shoot.
  - o Knocking the ball slightly to the side.

- o   Accelerating onto it.
  - o   Setting the non-kicking foot to the side of the ball.
  - o   Arms for balance.
  - o   Head over the ball.

- Shooting.
  - o   Striking with the laces or instep.
  - o   Smooth follow through.

Development:

- Limit the number of touches in the shooting half of the pitch.

Soccer Drill: Loads of goals.

A fun, somewhat chaotic drill which is guaranteed to get the players excited, while working on their accuracy of shooting. It is an excellent drill to use at the end of a warmup, to expel all the excess energy with which seven, eight, nine and ten year olds are blessed and get them ready for a focussed session to follow.

Use With: Any age, but the drill is particularly effective with this age range because they are old enough to strike the ball with sufficient pace for the drill to work, but young enough to be excited by the prospect of scoring into an empty goal.

Objectives: Shoot through a small gate which is operating as a goal.

Equipment: Cones to make goals. Plenty of balls. Cones to mark out shooting lines.

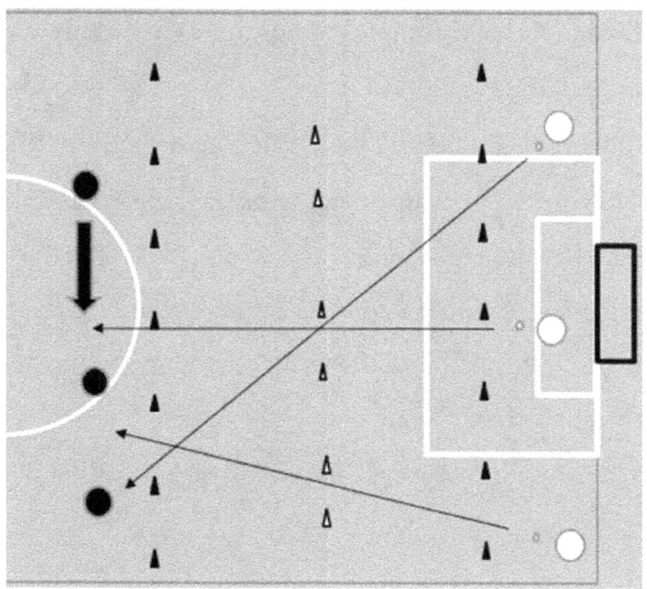

Operation of Drill:

- Set up the drill. It is very simple. Mark out two lines of cones ten to twenty metres apart (depending on the ability of your players to strike the ball). These are the shooting lines.

- In the middle of these lines create three small gates using two cones three metres apart. These are the goals.

- Divide the players into two groups. Give each player in one of the groups a ball.

- Players move behind their respective shooting lines.

- They must shoot through the gates from behind their shooting line.

- Each successful goal is one point, but only if the ball is hit with sufficient power to reach the opponent's shooting line.

- Their opponents then shoot back once a ball reaches them.

Key Skills:

- Striking with firmness and accuracy.
- Controlling the ball.

Development:

- Use just one gate in the middle, meaning players have to develop shooting at an angle.
- Or allow only two touches before shooting. One to control, one to set the ball for the shot.
  - o This is particularly useful with more able players because they will realise that if they can shoot at an angle, they will create an even harder angle for their opponents to shoot back. This will help to translate into shooting for the far post in a real match situation.

Soccer Drill: Unfair Sides

This is a rondo style drill which helps players work together to create shooting opportunities. It is a fast paced drill, which works extremely well but does require a bit of understanding from the players, so it may take a couple of attempts to get the drill working. Although a rondo, so the sides are unbalanced, it presents a match like scenario in that there is some opposition to the attacking side.

Use With: Any age. The youngest children will need time to understand their various roles.

Objectives: Work as a team to create a shooting opportunity.

Equipment: Small pitch (a half sized match pitch works well) with a goal at each end. Balls. Bibs.

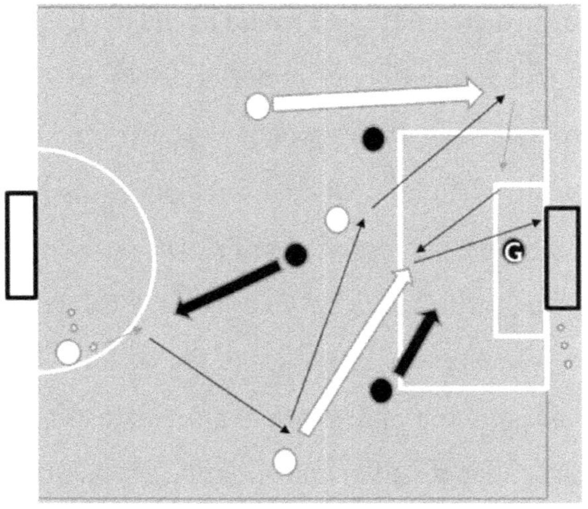

Operation of Drill:

- Create two teams of four.

- Have a number of balls at each end for speed of play.

- Teams alternate between defense and attack.

- Attacks involve all four players of a team.

- Defense involves two players and a goalkeeper, so there is one spare player whose job can be to make sure there are enough balls on either side of their goal for the drill to continue.

- Rolls rotate after each round of the drill. This is the bit that young players may find tricky to understand, but with practice it will come to them.

- The drill begins with one of the attacking sides dribbling a ball onto the pitch. The balls are lined up just behind the goal lines so play can begin from anywhere across the width of the pitch.

- Make sure the player who starts rotates. It might be worth keeping a list and shouting out the name of the player to begin. Young children have a highly defined sense of fairness, and if it is the same player too often who begins, the drill can quickly deteriorate into arguments.

- The four attackers move towards the other goal and seek to create a shooting opportunity.

- Play continues until either a goal is scored or the ball goes out of play.

- Meanwhile the defense tries to stop them.

- Each time, there are two defenders, a goalkeeper and one player 'out'. Again, roles rotate each play.

Key Skills:

- Working as a team to create a shooting opportunity.
- Communication.
- Passing, dribbling.
- Shooting effectively.

Development:

- Add a third defender, so outfield the attack is 4 v 3.

Soccer Drill: Shooting Across the goal.

A fast and simple drill which helps players to understand that often it is best to shoot across the goal, aiming for the far post.

Use With: Any age.

Objectives: Shoot across the goal.

Equipment: Cones to mark starting lines and to split the goal in half. Goal and balls.

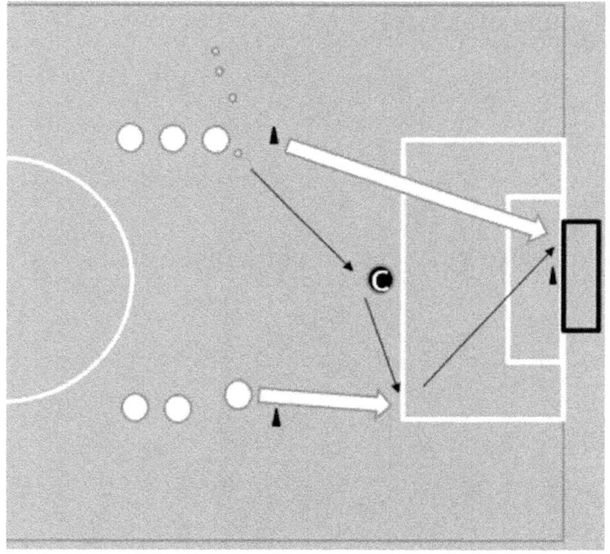

Operation of Drill:

- Place two cones in line with the edge of the penalty area, and ten metres back from it.

- Place the balls by one of the cones.

- Place the other cone in the centre of the goal. Players use this to help them aim for the far post.

- Split the players into two groups. One group behind each of the cones.

- The drill begins with the front player passing into the coach, who is standing centrally on the edge of the box.

- This player, and the front player from the other line, advance.

- The coach lays the ball off to either side.

- The player controls the ball and shoots aiming for the far post.

- His partner must follow the ball in, scoring himself or herself if they can reach the ball.

- The player who did NOT make the first pass collects the ball and takes it back with them.

- Players return to the side in which they started.

- When the drill has run through so every player has made an initial pass, swap the players over so they can have a round passing from the opposite side of the pitch.

Key Skills:

- Passing firmly into a target player (the coach).
- Shooting firmly across the goal.
- Supporting a teammate by making a run towards goal ready to pick up rebounds or shoot themself.

Development:

- Add a goalkeeper.

Soccer Drill: Who Can Shoot the furthest?

A drill which offers a fun way of getting technique for shooting ingrained and mastered. It is a short drill requiring very little equipment and can be a handy way of keeping players occupied and focussed whilst a fellow coach sets up another drill, perhaps one requiring more equipment.

Use With: All youth ages, from the very youngest to under twelves or even under thirteens.

Objectives: Strike the ball correctly, using the laces, for maximum power and distance.

Equipment: Balls, pitch.

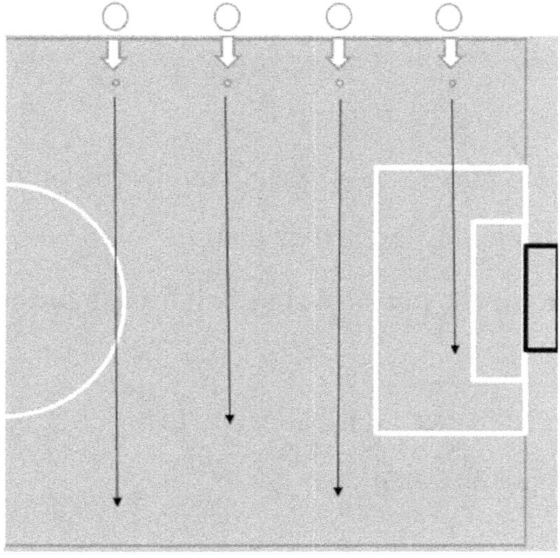

Operation of Drill:

- Each player beings with a ball.
- They spread along the touchline on side of the pitch, a little way back from the line itself.
- Coach does a sample shot to show technique:
  - Running onto the ball.
  - Arms for balance.
  - Non-kicking foot planted to side and slightly behind, as some lift will make the ball carry further.
  - Striking with the laces.
  - Head over the ball.
  - Smooth follow through.
- On the whistle players take a touch, run onto the ball, and strike it as far as they can.
- Winner is the player whose ball travels furthest from the line.
- Players retrieve their balls, and then shoot back from the opposite touchline.

Key Skills:

- Striking the ball correctly with the laces.
- Improving long distance shooting.

Development:

- Turn the drill into a fairground attraction by adding targets such as cones, water bottles and mannequins.

A key philosophy of this book is to make soccer fun. Hence the 'fairground stall' suggestion above. The following chapter offers five fun games which will not only help our players to develop skills, techniques, confidence, agility and a growing understanding of the game, but do so in a very enjoyable, entertaining way.

LEVEL 4 – CONTINUOUS IMPROVEMENT

Fun Games

Our children are very young, and so the following collection of small games seek to help players develop skills and understanding of the game, but in the context of a fun activity. As you will see, the names and themes are interchangeable and can easily be used them a name or theme that better fits your group of players.

Soccer Drill: Birthday Girl or Birthday Boy

This is a warmup drill which is a twist on Musical Chairs. It can be played on a player's birthday, with the player (if they wish) taking the role of the coach.

Use With: Under Sixes or below, Under Sevens, maybe younger Under Eights.

Objectives: React to a signal, shoot with accuracy

Equipment: Cones to mark out a circle. Cones to make small goals. Mini cymbals, or beater and box – anything which makes a loud noise and is hygienic to share among the players. (So, not a traditional whistle.)

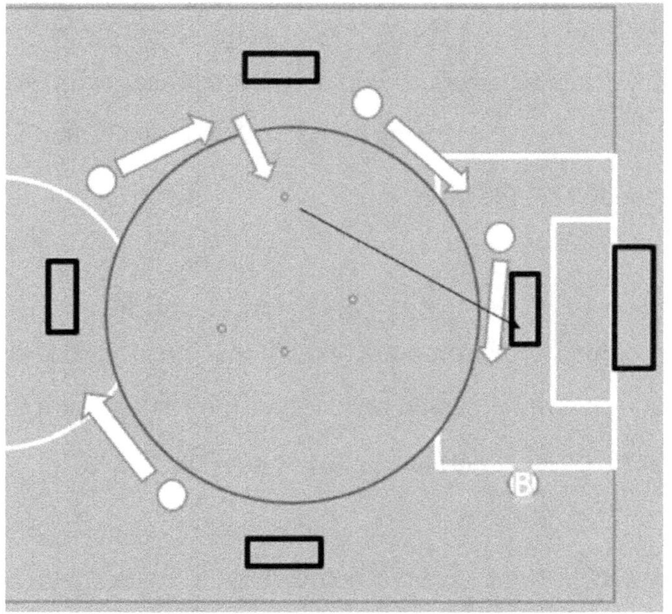

In the diagram above, the birthday child is represented by the 'B' in a white dot, but this could equally be the coach if the birthday celebrant wishes to join in the activity as a player.

Operation of Drill:

- Create a circle with a diameter of about 20 metres.
- Set up a number of cones, or use small goals, to set up goals outside of the circle, around five metres from the edge of the circle.
- Place enough balls in the circle for each player to have one.
- Players jog around the edge of the circle.
- The birthday player (or just the coach) has the noise making tool. He or she makes the sound after a few seconds.
- The players rush to the centre and shoot from within the circle to try to score a goal.
- First player to score wins that round. (Only if you wish to include a competitive element.)

Key Skills:

- Reacting quickly to a situation.
- Shooting with accuracy and speed.

Development:

- There are many ways to vary the game.
  - Have one less ball than players. After each round remove a ball and the player who did not shoot.
  - Have a scoring system, for example five points for the first goal, three for any goal scored that is the only score in that particular goal, one point if more than one player scores in the goal.
  - Instead of jogging round the circle, they dribble round it. On the sound, they dribble into the circle and attempt to score in their own goal.

Soccer Drill: Time for a Tidy Up

At first this seems like a simple drill but in fact it requires a lot of teamwork and deft skills. It is also great fun,

Use With: Any age.

Objectives: Develop weight of the pass (weighted pass). Do so by trying to clear balls from one zone to another, without kicking them out of bounds.

Equipment: Cones to mark out grid. Lots of balls.

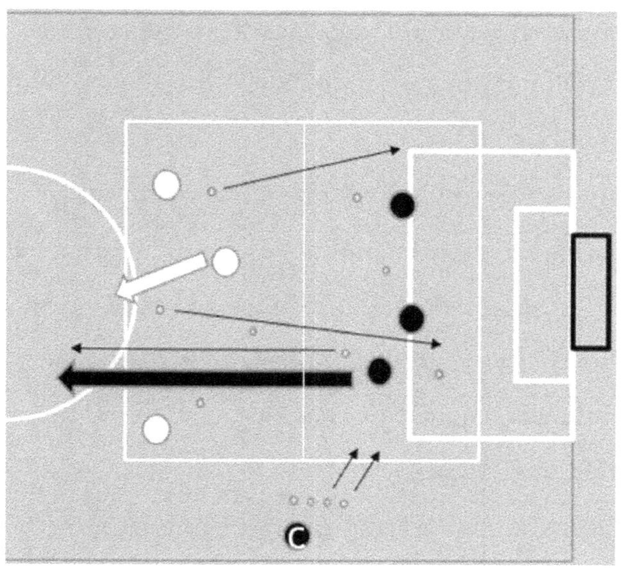

In the diagram, we see the coach kicking two additional balls in the black grid after a black player kicks his or her ball out of the playing zone. This player then runs to collect the ball they have kicked outside the zone.

Operation of Drill:

- Make a square grid around twenty metres by twenty metres. (Or use a penalty area by playing across it. Or, for a more challenging drill, make a grid which is wider than it is long.)
- Divide the grid in half with a line of cones.
- Divide the players into two groups. The game works best with three a side to five a side but can work with slightly larger groups. It does not matter is there are an uneven number of players and so one side has an additional player.
- Start with four balls in each side of the grid.
- Have a large collection of spare balls.
- The aim is to pass all of the balls into the opponents' half of the grid.

- If a ball leaves the grid, then the last player to touch the ball must retrieve it and return it to the coach (temporarily taking them out of the game).

- Meanwhile, the coach kicks two balls back into the grid of the offending player.

- Quite often it will not be possible for either side to completely clear their grid, so set a time limit (about three minutes for Under Sixes, up to five minutes for Under Eights).

- Give a countdown for the last ten seconds.

- The game ends when either one side has cleared their balls into the other half of the grid, or on time when the whistle blows. Whichever side has fewer balls in the grid at that moment is the winner.

- Always have a replay!

Key Skills:

- Passing accurately, tactically and with good weight.
- Working out strategies to win the game.
- Teamwork to employ the strategies.

Development:

- Add to the mayhem by placing one opposing player into the other team's grid. Their aim to prevent balls crossing into their own team's half.

Soccer Drill: Bombs away

This is an action packed drill with numerous variations easily applied. It works on both dribbling and passing skills. However, be firm with players to keep the ball on the ground at all times to avoid injury.

Use With: Under Sixes to Under Tens. Younger ages perhaps lack the coordination to play the game safely, while older players may hit the ball too firmly for it to be completely safe.

Objectives: Dribble with skill, speed and awareness. Side foot pass with accuracy.

Equipment: Cones for grid. Plenty of balls.

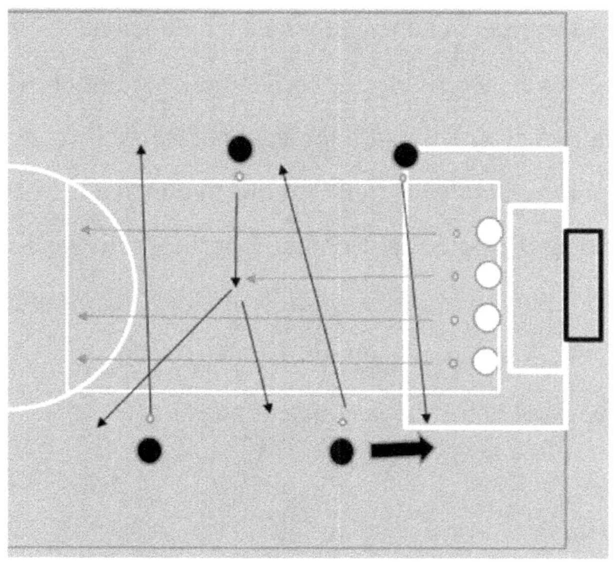

Operation of Drill:

- Create a grid thirty metres long by ten metres wide.

- Divide the group into two teams.

- Each player has a ball.

- The aim is for one team to dribble the ball from end of the grid to the other.

- Meanwhile the other team attempt to 'bomb' their opponent's ball with their own by side foot passing in.

- The bombers can use any ball which leaves the grid. However, for safety they must make sure the ball is stationary and outside the grid before kicking it (kicking a moving ball is more like to see it lift, giving the potential to hit and hurt a dribbler).
- Each player who successfully makes it from one end to the other scores a point for their team.
- Swap roles for the second round.

Key Skills:

- Dribbling both using the laces to run with the ball, and with close control to avoid balls hitting their own ball.
- Pass with accuracy to hit a moving target, using the side-foot technique.

Development:

- Rather than two large teams, make a number of smaller teams.

- Bibs to identify teams.

- They take it in turns to run the gauntlet of bombs fired from all other teams working together.

Soccer Drill: Last Man (or Woman) Standing

A variation on the drill above. This is an individual drill rather than a team drill and makes for a good warm up activity. It works in any shaped grid, but a circular one is best as it prevents players winning by hiding in a corner.

Use With: Any age.

Objectives: Dribble with control within a crowded area.

Equipment: Grid – diameter approximately twenty metres. Balls

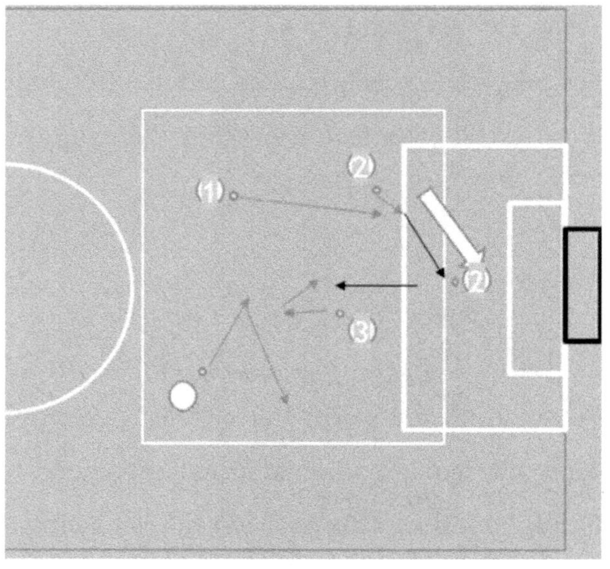

In the diagram above we see player one dribbling to player two and kicking their ball out of play. Player two then runs to where their ball is lying and attempts to hit player three's ball.

Operation of Drill:

- Create the circular (or square, rectangular or any other shaped) grid. Size depends on numbers and skill level of players. The better the players, the smaller the grid.
- Each player has a ball.
- They find a space within the grid.
- On the whistle they must dribble around within the grid.
- Meanwhile any player can attempt to kick any other player's ball out of the grid.
- Once out, the player can continue to participate by kicking any ball outside of the grid to hit the ball of a dribbler. (Same rules as for Bombs Away, for the same safety reasons).
  - A player may retrieve a spare ball in the grid, but they must not interfere with any dribbler until they are outside the grid, when they may place the ball and attempt to pass it to hit a dribbler's ball.)

- A player is out if…
    - They lose control and their ball leaves the grid.
    - They commit a foul in the coach's opinion.
    - Their ball is kicked out of the grid by an opponent.
    - Their ball is hit by any other ball, both from outside the grid or by touching the ball of another dribbler.
    - They stand still for more than two seconds.

Key Skills:

- Dribbling with the ball under close control.
- Passing with accuracy to hit a moving target.

Development:

- Introduce tacklers, whose only aim is to kick the ball out of the grid.

Soccer Drill: Space Cadets versus Aliens

This is a rondo style drill, close to a match situation, made more fun with the idea that it is played between Space cadets and Aliens.

Use With: Any age up to about Under Tens, after which they might find the idea a little childish. However, the drill is still good, just without the aliens' and space cadets' themes.

Objectives: Play soccer to create goal scoring opportunities, and score goals, against an opposition with fewer players.

Equipment: Half pitch. Goal. Ball. Some masks??? Some names for the Aliens, e.g. Dalek, Martian etc? Some ranks for the Space Cadets – Captain, Engineer, Doctor? Work this depending on how you believe your group will respond.

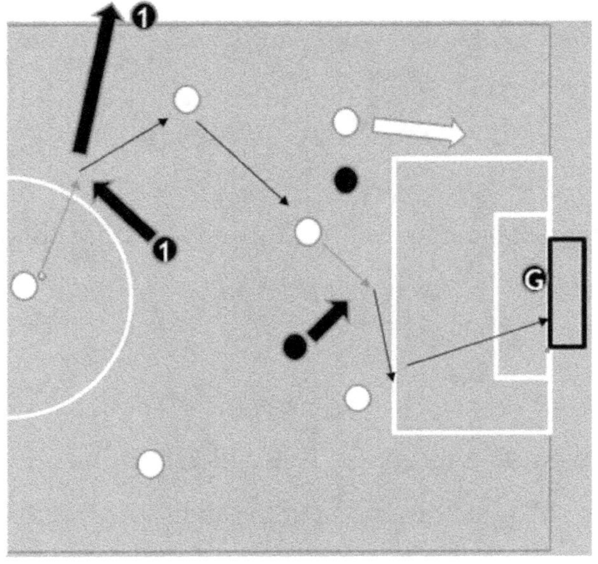

In the diagram, we see the white team – the Space Cadets – fashioning a chance and scoring. We then see defender 1, or Alien 1, leaving the field for the next round as a result of the goal.

- The drill is a match play Rondo, which begins six v three plus a keeper. Play on half a pitch, using the halfway line as the end line.

- The attackers, the Space Cadets, have one minute to fashion a shot against the Aliens, the defending side.

- If the Aliens can prevent a shot in the time allowed or force the Space Cadets to hit the ball out of play, or clear the ball over the end line, the Space Cadets lose a player.

- If they score, the Aliens lose a player.

- (If a shot is saved, the keeper can try to kick the ball over the end line or pass it to a fellow Alien to kick it out).

- The next round is ten seconds shorter.

- Each round, rotate the players who are off, but keep the numbers as they should be.

- If at any point there are the same number of outfield Aliens as attackers, the Aliens win, if all Aliens are eliminated the Space Cadets survive (i.e. win), and if all six rounds are played, the team which won most rounds are the winners.

Key Skills:

- Teamwork and communication.
- Accurate passing and shooting.
- Decision making.

Development:

- To keep all players active, rather than a player being eliminated they change sides depending on the outcome.
- When the number of outfield Aliens matches the Space Cadets, the Aliens become the attackers.

With a little creativity, pretty much any drill can be turned into a fun game. One that does not have to be overly competitive (for every winner, there are usually multiple losers), and whilst that might – unfortunately (unless you are one of the regular winners) be a fact of life – it is not a lesson which has to be learned by the age of eight. Nevertheless, games make learning fun, and fun offers the best way to learn.

Soccer Drill: Cops and Robbers

A variation on a common fun game, adapted to the Under 6 age range.

Use With: Any age, the example here is specifically geared towards younger children.

Objectives: The players are the robbers; they have each stolen a ball which they must dribble from the club store (narrow side of the grid) to home (the opposite side of the grid). The coach, or another adult, is the Cop. They must capture the robbers by tackling them or forcing them to dribble or kick the ball out of the grid. Once 'captured', the former robbers become new cops.

Equipment: Lots of balls.

Operation of Drill:

- Create a grid approximately 20 metres x 30 metres.
- The aim is for players (robbers) to dribble from one side of the grid to the other without being tackled by a 'cop'.
- When a player is tackled, or dribbles out of the grid, they kick their ball away and become a cop.
- Last robber to be caught is the winner.

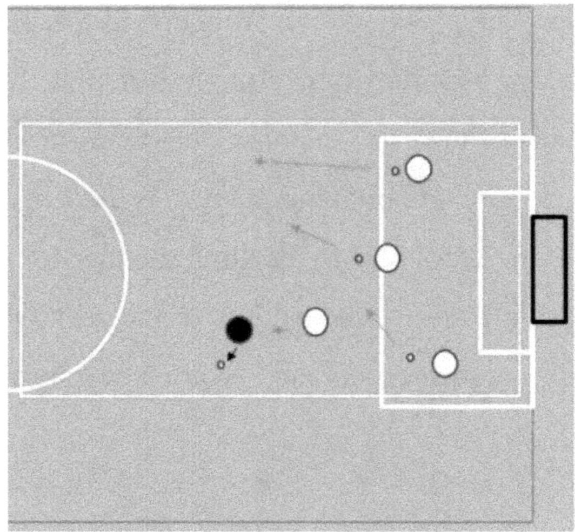

Key Skills: Our focus here is not to instil complex instructions but to let the children learn for themselves the best way to do well in the game. As coaches, we give just three instructions:

- Keep your heads up on the lookout for cops – helps players to develop an awareness of the wider game.
- Use small touches of the ball to get round the cops without being caught (tackled).
- Kick the ball further in front of you to accelerate away and escape.

Development:

- A great benefit of this game is that by the coach joining in, he or she can determine which players are going to be tackled first, thus letting the less able players to get more goes without being caught, thus raising their self-esteem when they 'escape' from the 'cop'.

Soccer Drill: Grandma or Grandpa Goalie.

This game uses the traditional children's game of Grandmother's Footsteps and works really well both indoors and out.

Use With: Up to Under Tens.

Objectives: React quickly. Shoot with power and accuracy. Improve judgement of when to shoot.

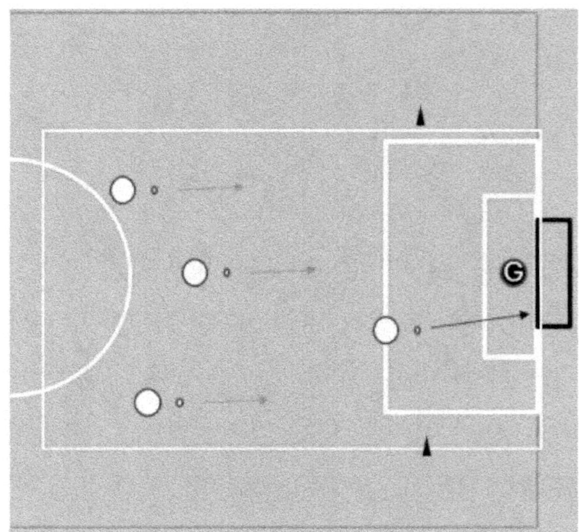

The winner is the first player or the players to score a goal.

Equipment: Lots of balls. One goal.

Operation of Drill:

- Mark out a large rectangular grid or use the width of a pitch.
- Place a goal at one end.
- Place two cones ten metres from the goal, to create the shooting line.
- Players begin at the opposite end of the grid.
- The Goalie stands in the goal with their back to the players. Initially the coach or a helper is the Goalie, but as players improve, another player can take on this role.
- They dribble towards the goal with the ball under close control.
- The goalie, with their back still to the players, shouts '4,3,2,1 Ha Ha' turning on 'Ha Ha'. Any player who

is not standing still, with their foot on the ball must go back to the beginning and start again.

- The goalie turns back to face the other way, and the players continue to advance. Next time, it is just '3,2,1 Ha Ha' before turning.
- However, when players think they are close enough to score, they can shoot. If they miss, or the goalie saves it, again they must start from the beginning again.
- They are not permitted to get closer than the shooting line (although they can shoot from further away if they wish).

Key Skills:

- Close control to give the best chance of stopping during the countdown.
- Shooting accurately.
- Judging the best time to shoot.

Development:

- The coach, as grandma or grandpa goalie, can judge the speed of their call to increase or decrease the amount of time players have to control their ball.

Soccer Drill: When it Rains Too Hard

We've all been there. The best laid plans. The perfect session ready to go, disrupted by any manner of unforeseen events. A sudden, dramatic change in the weather means it is unsafe to stay outside, and the First Team have bagged the sports hall (if you are lucky enough to have access to one). You mistime the final activity and complete your plenary five minutes early. You arrive ready to go and the previous practice is over running. The team is too young to be left to chat among themselves, and a bad start (or end) to the session is hard to recover from.

Here are a couple of well-tried and successful games which work perfectly indoors or outdoors and require no equipment beyond a bit of space for our players to wave their arms on the spot.

Use With: Any age ranges from Under-fives to Under thirteens. They are ideal with five- to eleven-year-olds, but twelve years olds love them too.

Objectives: It would be pushing it to suggest these games will develop much in the way of soccer skills. However, because they are fun, they help promote group unity, and because they require focus, concentration and, in one case, dexterity, they do help with our players' development.

Equipment: None

Operation of Games:

- Game One – 'Do This, Do That'

- Coach leads this.

- Rather like the game of 'Simon Says,..' the coach makes a movement, such as raising an arm.

- If this is accompanied by the words 'Do this' the players copy the movement. If the coach says 'Do that' they stay in their previous position. They sit down if they move on a 'Do that' instruction.

- The coach moves through changes quickly, depending on the age of the children. Equally, whilst we might expect a twelve-year-old to avoid even a twitch on a 'Do that', we can allow more movement from a six-year-old.

Game Two – 'Ninety-Nine'

- One player is 'on'. They stand at the front with their eyes closed and their back to the rest of the group.

- The coach picks on a player who says 'Ninety-nine' in a disguised voice.

- The 'on' player turns, looks at the group, and tries to identify the speaker,
- If correct, they have another turn, if wrong they are replaced by the speaker.

Key Skills:

- Focus
- Reaction time.

Development:

- After getting a couple right, try having two people speak simultaneously to fool the player who is on.

Playing Through the Winter

Soccer is an outdoor sport. The growth of indoor facilities, and variations like futsal have made it certainly easier for coaches to keep going with the development of their young players when the weather turns. Plus, of course, they are a bonus for parents seeking to keep their children active and interested through the long evenings and chilly weekends.

But a kickaround in the park with their parents, or grandparents, or shooting at the wall or goal in the back yard are not practical options when winter arrives, at least not when the (increasingly) extreme weather hits. So, in this chapter we will offer some 'indoor' options to keep our under sixes (and indeed, most of these activities work well with any young player) busy, active and improving their soccer skills and knowledge.

There are no diagrams in this chapter. It's best to design your games around the spaces you have available.

Soccer Drill: Hand Golf

Let's go back to basics for a moment. What skills and techniques – physical and mental – do we require to become a good soccer player? In answering we are going to ignore our feet. Which leaves factors such as balance, head position and hand-eye coordination. On the mental strength side we can add resilience alongside a willingness to practise?

Whilst we might not want our six-year-old kicking a soccer ball around our lounge, or even in the hallway, we can both entertain and develop our daughter or son's physical coordination and mental strength with simple, fun games. Playing with our child will develop their enthusiasm when the weather mitigates against the appeal of the outdoors, and soon we may well find that they are developing their own similar games, not only occupying themselves but also helping to develop their social skills (where friends or siblings are involved), ingenuity and self-reliance.

The game here is golf based, but there are many alternatives we can create and adapt which, like this, pretty much require only the bits and pieces most people have lying around the house.

Use With: Any age.

Objectives: Get the ball from the 'tee' (a piece of card) to the 'hole' (a wastepaper bin or plastic container) in as few shots as possible.

Equipment:

Ball – Small, golf ball sized and lightweight. A ping pong ball is perfect, but even a tightly screwed wad of paper, wound round with sticky tape, will work.

Hole – Waste bins set around the house, or old ice cream containers (not ideal with a ping pong golf ball as the ball may bounce out), plastic jugs or plastic fizzy drink bottles with the tops cut off and perhaps weighted with a few coins.

Tees – Simple cards explaining where the hole is located, and a 'par' target number of shots. Bunkers, roughs and fairways – put obstacles on the route, a freestanding clothes dryer, tall lamps, small tables etc; but also create clear areas on the best route to act as the 'fairway'.

Score Card (optional) – Create your own score card and print out - a simple table such as below is perfect (and even helps our child with basic number bonding…):

HOLE	PAR	YOUR SCORE	+ or _
1	3		
2	5		
3	4		

Operation of Drill:

- Set up the course. Use multiple rooms in the house to add to the challenge.

- Prepare the tee cards (you could use sticky notes for the par number and location to allow you to re-use the cards).

- The first shot – the tee shot – is a one-handed throw – under arm for accuracy or overarm for distance. Future shots require the ball to be scooped and flicked using the fingers, played from its stopping position. When within five large steps of the hole, the player can 'putt'. Here they go onto one knee and throw the ball underarm into the hole.

Key Skills:

- Strategy to reach the hole most easily.
- Hand eye coordination.
- Balance when propelling the ball – head still for accuracy, legs slightly apart and non-throwing arm slightly out for balance.

Development:

- Play a four-round tournament.

Soccer Drill: Creating an Indoor Space Outdoors

The games and drills suggested elsewhere in this chapter are great fun and will develop important physical and mental skills for our young players. But, with the best will in the world, they are not soccer. Because, let us be honest, as much as we adore little Adel, love little Lewis, we don't want them kicking a ball in our house. Understandably. We might sometimes be able to overcome this problem if we can utilise an outside space, especially if it is covered. If windows, furniture or tools might be damaged by a wayward shot then replace the soccer ball with a beach ball. The skills required are the same.

Use With: Any age.

Objectives: The game here uses targets drawn with chalk on a wall. Commercial products are available which will do the same job, but they are expensive and we do not need them.

Equipment: Ball. Area of hard standing, ideally covered (such as a long porch, car standing area or relatively clear garage). You may need to move the car out of the garage if necessary.

Operation of Drill:

- Draw targets on the wall. Circles or squares approximately one metre in diameter are good. Make them smaller for older or more able players, larger for beginners. Some should be at ground level.
- Play the ball against the wall. One point for hitting the wall, three points for hitting a floor level target, six points for one off the ground.
- Move to control the returning ball. Two touches allowed plus one to stop the ball dead.
- Continue from where the ball stops dead.
- The round ends when the ball isn't stopped in the permitted number of touches or misses the wall.

Key Skills:

- Balance for striking the ball.
- Quick movement and anticipation to control the returning ball.
- Good first touch

Development:

- Add numbers in the targets, higher numbers for harder targets to hit.
- This game can also be good for goalkeepers.
- Here set a mark 10 metres from the wall.
- Players must throw the ball to hit the target.
- They move quickly to catch the rebound.
- They return to the mark and go again, aiming for a different target.

Soccer Drill: Balloon Soccer Tennis

This is a great activity for indoors. Not much space is needed and there is minimal risk of any damage to ornaments or (even more importantly…) players. A bit of careful moving of our aunt's expensive glassware might be prudent, depending on the layout and space of the room.

Use With: Any age.

Objectives: Use kicking skills to win points as in tennis.

Equipment: Balloons. A 'net'. A series of weighted plastic bottles, a narrow occasional table, the garden badminton net, brought in for winter and tied to a couple of chairs, some storage cartons placed upside down on the floor…whatever can create an obstacle without causing harm to itself or players.

Operation of Drill:

- Serve by placing the balloon on the floor and kicking it over the net.
- Receiver has two touches to stop the balloon and return it using whatever part of the body is allowed in soccer.
- The balloon is permitted to bounce once before playing or be volleyed/chested etc before it hits the ground.

- The balloon is out if, before touching the ground, it hits the ceiling, a wall or a piece of furniture.

- Score as per tennis.

- For younger players allow them to catch the ball and then volley it back.

Key Skills:

- Balance

- Technique to propel the balloon.

- Anticipation

Development:

- Increase or decrease the touches allowed depending on the skill level of the player.

- Create other balloon games.

- Create a balloon skills course – for example ten juggles: ten penalties to land on the sofa; throw, chest, turn and shoot.

Soccer Drill: Commercial Small Training Equipment

There are a number of commercial indoor training items available online or in sports shops. Most work on the theme of a ball attached to elastic, limiting how far it will travel, and returning it to the kicker. They do require a bit of space and can be expensive.

Soccer Drill: Using the Imagination

Board and practical games are perhaps not as popular as they used to be. However, they still exist and can provide hours of entertainment whilst fostering and maintaining our children's love of soccer during the times when actually playing the sport might be impractical.

Use With: Any relevant age – most games have age guidance.

Objectives: As per the game.

Equipment: Games such as Subbuteo are ideal. However, there are many other tabletop soccer games available, including the free standing, rod-based games we find in amusement arcades. Where parents are happy, online games such as FIFA or Football Manager can help to foster a real love and interest for the sport. They are quite addictive, though.

In addition, there are countless dice games, drill dice and soccer themed board games which will help to both foster and build on our children's natural enthusiasm for the sport.

Operation of Drill:

- Follow the rules of the particular game.

Key Skills:

- Developing wider interest in soccer, which will encourage them to investigate more about the game, such as watching matches on TV and online, reading and talking about the sport.
- When the weather improves enough to get outside again, their love and enthusiasm will be as high as ever.

Development:

- There are a few downsides to the suggestions in this activity. Not least among these is the cost associated with purchasing commercially made games and software. We also get into the much-discussed area of overuse of screens and their impact on the social development of young minds and bodies.
- However, young children are not so different at heart to we were, or are parents were, when we were that age. Their imaginations are strong and given the

right encouragement and stimulus we all know that our children will create some terrific games of their own, which will occupy them for long periods.

- So, how about purchasing some miniature plastic soccer balls and encouraging them to create their own soccer pitch? Parents may need to help with the goals – Lego© or the equivalent works well but they will soon get the idea. They can then play matches using their other toys. Their toy soldiers or other figures; toy cars perhaps.

- Buy some of those little bags of round chocolate balls, and suggest every time they score a goal, or a 'goalie' makes a great save, they can eat the ball. (They'll soon get the idea of not scoring too many goals too easily…or the game ends far too soon.)

- Get them to set up skill courses using other toys.

- The benefits include all of those mentioned in the main part of this activity – along with the creativity bonus which comes with building their own field of play. The cost is substantially lower.

Off the Field Development

The children we are coaching are developing quickly – physically, emotionally, cognitively and socially. Their involvement in soccer can only help our players in their progression – in all respects. Whilst it might seem that there are few links between, say, physical development and cognitive development, in fact there are many. So many factors influence the connection in the brain which lead to improved cognitive function. Self-esteem, nurture, physical health – the list goes on.

We can encourage our players to use their love of soccer away from their drills and their matches. We can encourage their physical development by encouraging to play other sports, run around, be active.

We can stress the importance of eating a varied and healthy diet. A rainbow of colours in their food will help to keep them fit and healthy. We can develop their reading enthusiasm and ability – with all emotional and intellectual benefits this brings – by encouraging them to read soccer books, fact and fiction, get a soccer magazine, read programmes from their local clubs.

We can help them to develop concentration skills by encouraging them to watch matches on TV. Edited highlights, or snippets online perhaps to begin with, but if we can capture their imagination, whole games will soon follow. We can encourage their social development by encouraging groups to play together at the park (with parental oversight, of course), to try out the drills they are learning in training sessions, for example. We can encourage them to learn about the sport they are growing to love, thus developing their intellectual curiosity and metacognitive learning. These will pay huge dividends in our players' schooling, which in turn will raise their confidence and self-esteem, making them better decision makers, more confident and therefore better players of the beautiful game.

If we see ourselves that the weekly training sessions, and the matches we play are just a part of our players' soccer learning journey, we will engender the same enthusiasm in our boys and girls, with all the benefits this brings for their soccer, their schooling, their general well-being, happiness and development.

There are also a number of ideas we can try out ourselves to make it easier for our players to flourish in off the field activities. The remainder of this chapter will focus on these.

Admittedly, most likely, we see our players for an hour a week during the coaching session, maybe for another hour or so at weekends when we have our match. The remainder of the time, we may seem to have little direct input into their soccer development. So while we have little direct input into our players' progress off the field, we can influence it, and not just through the points made above. The fact that the children come to soccer training, have joined a club or a team, means the game is one of their biggest interests. If they are loving our training sessions, looking forward to matches, getting their chance to play in a supportive, encouraging environment, then that interest will grow and grow. They will play soccer in the playground during their break times, certainly with and maybe without our encouragement meet up with mates for a kick about in the garden or park. Get mum and dad to be their goalkeeper while they shoot at the garden goal, persuaded grandad to take them and their siblings to the park for a kick around, even perhaps beg mum, or dad or older brother or sister to take them to a real, live game in a real, live, buzzing stadium.

As coaches we can tap into this enthusiasm and offer to parents, to schools, to the community, to our players the opportunity to improve their soccer development off the field and away from formal practices.

Not every one of the suggestions which follow will work for all coaches, or all communities, or for all players. But as we get to know these aspects of our lives, we can pick, choose and adapt ways to take our soccer training beyond the one or two hours per week we get to directly influence our young soccer players.

The following list is presented in no particular order. However, it does help our players to develop many of the key attributes of a soccer player. Again, in particular order of importance these include acquiring skills and techniques, developing understanding of the game, developing agility, balance and coordination in the wider sense plus the development of self-esteem and social skills.

Looking after Ourselves

Before we start to look at ways in which we can assist children in their off the field development, a short word about our own off the field development. Or, more precisely, well-being. This section is really aimed more at those looking to begin a coaching commitment, as more experienced coaches will already be aware of the risks.

The fact is that being a coach is great. Especially with children. And despite the additional challenges of coaching seven, eight, nine and ten year olds, the rewards really do make it worthwhile. We will get to know our players, become involved in their lives, get to know their parents, spend hours each week preparing sessions and getting ready for games, that on top of the actual delivery of our drills and organising our teams for matches. There will be times when we will be as untrained counsellors, unqualified (beyond a very important first aid course) nurses, teachers who have never been through teacher training. We will make mistakes, which will haunt us. And we will get much more right which, being human, we will enjoy for a short while before moving on.

All of this equates to a large time and emotional commitment. Often a financial one too. There are few coaches who do not dig into their own pockets when a piece of equipment is needed, or balls become short, or the pump breaks, or the team do well and are deserving of a doughnut or burger or packet of sweets. With our younger children, we are unlikely to be funded if we prepare sticker charts, or buy this book or that magazine, or sign up to one of the numerous online drill websites, some of which are very good, some less so.

So it is important that when considering how we can help our players with their off field development, we also consider the time commitment we can make, in the light of our family, work and financial commitments, and in terms of its impact on our other interests. A tired, stress coach earning the ire of their partner or children is not going to be at their best when it comes to running coaching sessions.

Going to a game

There is nothing to beat it. The atmosphere, the noise, the smell. The thrill of our team scoring, even the irrational over reaction of a defeat. Some of our players will already attend live matches with parents, grandparents and so forth. Most though, will not have done so yet. Professional clubs are commercial enterprises, they need people through their turnstiles. In particular, young people. Because catch a child young, and they become supporters for life, and thus a source of income. Gate receipts, memberships and merchandising are essential income streams for a professional set up.

Therefore, most clubs will offer special deals – sometimes for any game, sometimes for particular matches where the stadium is unlikely to sell out – for young supporters, and for clubs. Why not organise a trip to a game? Hire a minibus, get a couple of adult helpers on board and head off?

Or in the club's newsletter write a short article publicising the incentives on offer from a local professional club.

Helping at a school

Work patterns are changing, there is no doubt about this. Many nations introduced work from home schemes during the pandemic, and whilst many people are back at the office, or in the sales room or wherever now, working patters are undoubtedly more flexible. All the better for it, most would say. People work a day or two per week from home, their hours are, where possible more flexible.

A very rewarding way of spending an afternoon a week – just a couple of hours will be appreciated – is to approach a school as a volunteer. If we select the local primary or elementary school, there is a good chance we will come across some of our players, and to see them operate in a different environment will help our understanding of getting the best from them. We will also pick up tips and techniques from watching teachers in action. We can all learn from each other. Of course, as well as benefits to ourselves as coaches, the learning we experience ourselves will help our coaching and improve the outcomes for our players.

Or we can offer our particular skill set. We can lead coaching sessions or after school clubs in soccer, giving a wider range of opportunities to both our own players, and other children who may well, as a result of attending our lessons or club, look to join a team out of school with all the benefits this will bring.

Offering training to teachers

Making a weekly commitment may be beyond our capacity, but we can also assist our players' – and their peers' – development by offering to train teachers. Many elementary schools do not have the resources to offer in-school extra-curricular clubs and lessons, although the benefits of sport on academic learning are beyond question. Some will make the commitment to bring in outside coaches and the benefit they offer is huge. However, they are also expensive. Whereas we are free. We can give some enthusiastic teachers and assistants guidance and tips on coaching soccer, which they can turn into regular lessons or weekly club sessions. Again, the real benefit lies in the out of school development of children.

Education is finally encompassing so much about how learning styles among children differ. And this includes non-learning, where children (most often boys) become disillusioned with the system and effectively opt out of it. We will not see this too much among our age range, but certainly by ages ten or eleven there are a growing number of school refusers, truants and those who will not engage with the system. It is a developmental stage that, sadly, many enter and few grow out of. Whole lifetimes will be impacted by this – qualifications, careers, financial health, relationships and children who are excluded from school are far more likely to end up in the criminal justice system than their peers who, as adults and teens, have the benefit of a solid education behind them.

Educationalists are learning that alternative styles of learning often help to ease this problem. One prominent alternative style is learning through sport.

Penalty shoot outs at fairs etc

Away from the heavy field of pedagogy there is a simple way of helping our, and other, children experience some soccer. A method which does not require a regular commitment and which will, with luck, see us outside involved in a fun event during the best of times weather wise. A method in which our families can also come along and have a good time. Clubs, schools, organisations, regions, villages, charities – so many hold fund raising events through fairs and fetes. Why not offer to run a penalty shoot-out competition? It can be a great money raiser and requires relatively little space and equipment, most of which as a coach we are likely to have access to as well.

Information sessions or leaflets for parents

The best way of aiding the off the field development of our players is to make use of their parents, grandparents and so forth. Newsletters are good ways of letting parents know what options are out there for their children, especially during school holidays and weekends. But a half termly information session can also be held, a chance for a chat, a drink and some sharing of information. We can team up with fellow coaches at other clubs to help share the workload. It is all for the benefit of our players.

Publicising Holiday training

Holiday sports and activity clubs are a growing field of the sports coaching market. Part childcare, part sporting opportunity, they vary in quality and cost. As with professional soccer clubs, this kind of activity club will see our soccer clubs as a useful, and free, source of publicity. Sometimes, it is possibly to haggle some equipment in return for, say, a successful leaflet drop.

Watching on TV

While most six year olds would find watching a full match on TV too long, we can encourage our young players to watch highlights programmes. This can help to encourage both an understanding of the game and help to develop the support of a particular team, which is likely to result in a lifelong engagement with the sport.

YouTube Challenges

A simple one this, set the group a challenge to master before the next session. Perhaps shooting with the outside of the foot or chipping the ball. Point the youngsters towards YouTube or other platforms' clips as a motivation and teaching tool.

Learn a skill challenge

In a similar vein, set players individual challenges to learn at home. These targets are most effective if they are SMART targets – with our age groups this can mean:

S = suitable for the age and ability of the player.

M = measurable for example, running with the ball between two points twenty metres apart in ten seconds, or scoring a goal with ten shots out of fifteen attempts.

A = achievable. No point setting a target which the player has little chance of achieving. They will simply become bored with the challenge, and reluctant to take on this sort of target in the future. Success is important.

R = reasonable. Consider the possibility of the player being able to undertake the challenge. If they have only a very small back yard, long passing drills are not going to work. Once more, so much of this comes back to knowing our players.

T = time sensitive. A well targeted challenge is aimed at an individual or a group, should be something they can, with a little practice, achieve within their normal routines and should take some aspect of their soccer playing experiences forward.

A good but simple example can be to set our players the task of learning to do multiple juggles, the number geared to their ability levels and age.

This is:

Suitable – because it is safe and does not require parental observation.

Measurable – we set them, say, five or eight or ten juggles.

Achievable – although it will take a bit of practice.

Reasonable – because we have geared the challenge to the players' own abilities.

Time sensible – because our players can get out and practise when they have a few moments to spare.

Taking up other sports

Sometimes, but thankfully less so these days, coaches can be a little insular about their sports. But a sports player will enjoy many different types of sport, and some, if not most, of the skills and techniques of those sports will be transferable to soccer. The vast range of social and self-esteem benefits any sport offers will help the development of our players' soccer performance.

Where we encourage players to take up other sports, show an interest in their progress and their stories, we will be helping both their own personal development and their soccer development. We can do this where we talk about and celebrate our own other sporting interests.

Getting parents, grandparents etc involved with the game themselves

The biggest motivation for young players to develop their sporting interests and soccer skills is the involvement of the people central to their lives. Parents, grandparents, siblings. There are so many variations of soccer now available fitting all ages, abilities, gender and availability. Futbol is well developed as in indoor sport in many countries around the world. Traditional indoor five a side continues to thrive in any community large enough to have a sports hall. All weather surfaces are becoming ever more prominent – and improving in quality. Six a side leagues are flourishing as a result. Walking soccer for the older, physically more fragile players, is a tremendous sport, providing a similar range of social benefits to older players as coaches can offer to their under sixes, sevens and eights. As coaches, we are likely to be and be seen as a central source of information about these varieties of the game. We can share this information to the benefit of our own players as well as their relations.

Reward 3:

As a reward for completing this chapter, I'd like to offer you my free book on "Soccer Mental Toughness". It's a book on skills, strategies and exercises to use your mind to improve performances on the field. Just scan the QR code to get your book.

One Team – Coach and Parents

Coach and parents – we're all in it for the same reasons. They are the development, enjoyment and well-being of our players. When we are working with children, and especially young children, these goals become even more important. Of course, parents are focussed primarily on their own children – that is how we humans are designed, so there's little point in trying to change it. Coaches, on the other hand, must take a more rounded approach. Whilst we are seeking to do the best for every player who comes to our sessions and who plays in our matches, we know that we cannot gear all of our time to the individual requirements of perhaps, ten, fifteen, twenty different players. Everybody's needs are different.

But we can set standards and expectations to make the relationship between coaches and parents the best it can be, and that in turn will serve the best interests of the young players in our team.

Below are five general qualities, rather than specifically soccer related ones, with which every parent will surely agree, and every coach will wish to promote:

- Make playing fun.
- Increase resilience to overcome setbacks.
- Build self-esteem to influence all aspects of life.
- Help children to learn the strength of team.
- Give players a voice (safeguarding mention)

If, at the end of a season, we can honestly say that we have helped every one of our players progresses in these five areas, then we can be rest assured that we are doing a good job. Crucially, though, they will be so much harder to achieve without the support of parents.

Let us look at each of these 'soft' aspects of a coach's role in more detail. Specifically, the way in which we can work with parents to deliver these goals in a manner which delivers the very best of outcomes for our players. Not only in their soccer, but in their wider lives as well.

One: Make Playing Fun

For children, the greatest enjoyment comes when they are active, when they are with friends, when they do not feel under pressure and, related to this, when they feel safe. With our Under Sixes, there is a likelihood that parents may well attend training sessions as well as matches and tournaments. We encourage parents to help to ensure fun is had by all when we create an atmosphere of positivity. This atmosphere contains a number of absolutes: no criticism if a player makes a mistake; no excessive encouragement which teeters on the edge of aggressive support; no challenging the coach over their decision making; no valuing of one player over another, irrespective of their ability level. As coach, we are in charge, and we can help foster the atmosphere we want with friendliness and smiles.

In the UK, where there is a well-developed and ingrained system of children's and youth soccer, many clubs have felt the need to impose upon parents a contract in an attempt to ensure their good behaviour. If necessary, this can be used to establish the atmosphere required, although if the same result can be achieved through example, rather than instruction, then that is better for all. It is almost always the case that when Mr Murray wishes to spend ten minutes every week explaining why his Michaela should really be playing centre forward, or Mrs Miller why young Mark is better up front than at the back they are doing so because of their love for their child. As frustrating as this might be, if we can deal with it with a smile so much the better.

Although, as coaches must also remember to ensure our soccer sessions are fun. Consider this true story. Two coaches, one from each team, are running the line during a match. Each constantly criticises the decisions of the other until, midway through the second half, matters reach such a head that a full-on fist fight occurs. The players, a little older than our target audience here, certainly did not find it fun. If the coach cannot set the example how can they expect their players, and their parents, to be at their best?

Two: Teach the resilience to overcome setbacks

Let us consider what kinds of setbacks our players are most likely to encounter. Within the context of their soccer, there are probably five which will occur most often:

- A sense that they have disappointed their parents, coach or teammates.
- The disappointment of losing a match.
- A sense that they are unable to conquer a skill or technique.
- A feeling that they have made a major soccer mistake.
- Falling out with a teammate.

We address these all in the same way. Through our own positivity. Children will only develop a sense that they have disappointed others if the reaction of others suggests this. This means that for us as coaches, we must train our mindset to ensure that the development of our players is our priority, not winning the league. Players will mimic our reactions. So, we applaud the effort rather than highlight the failure; we embody the attitude that not quite achieving our aim is a vital step along the road of getting better. The atmosphere we, and our players, engender, will communicate itself to our parents. They will self-govern the behaviour of newcomers to the group. Only in the rare example whereby a parent simply refuses to encourage and continues to criticise should we need to step in formally, firstly with a quiet word, then perhaps something in writing, and ultimately, exclusion from the training sessions and matches.

Our players will inevitably fall out from time to time. It is in our human DNA to promote ourselves first. That sense is stronger in children than adults, stronger still in younger children before society has had its chance to temper it. Flare ups occur and mostly, pass quickly. The coach can help by using distraction techniques such as telling the group to do ten star jumps or run to the nearest goal and back. Whatever has caused the disagreement will quickly pass, especially where coaches are successful in creating a positive environment.

The coach is the general who sets the tone, the parents are the soldiers who enforce it, the players are the locals who benefit. And, that benefit will not just be seen in their soccer, but in their wider lives. This leads neatly to the next quality parents and coaches work together to develop in our players.

Three: Build self-esteem to influence all aspects of life

There is little here that needs to be said. Self-esteem is the by-product of confidence. It is characterized by belief in oneself, a willingness to take measured risk and use falling short of our goal as a motivation to get better, rather than a reason to withdraw. Encouragement and reward are the fuels of this essential life skill, whilst criticism and sanction are its enemy. Given that parents love their children, and most will be aware that positivity is better than criticism, it begs the question as to why they do criticise. There are many reasons: frustration; a wish for their child to do better; a sense that they cannot moan at other people's children, but can at their own. Reflecting their own upbringing. It is probably true however that parental criticism of their child, or occasionally other children, almost always come from a belief that this is the best way to help their child. Of course, this is wrong. It is never the best way. As before, we model the behaviours we wish to see, we use the parental body to enforce this, and only when a parent fails to take the hint, and their behaviour will impact on the self-esteem of the players, do we step in. A quiet word, a longer word, formal action and ultimately, exclusion. We are excluding the parent, not the player, although the effect may, unfortunately, be the same.

Four: Help children to learn the strength of team

We mentioned earlier the egocentricity of the human animal, and how this is more pronounced in young children. We are helping our players to learn the vital life skill of valuing and respecting others when we promote the concept of 'team'. But, a six-year-old has very probably spent their entire existence, bar perhaps the beginning of their formal education, as the constant centre of their parents' lives. It is not surprising therefore that we will need the support of our parents to help our players to learn to value the team.

Yet the method for best achieving this does not change. Positivity and encouragements remain the keys. Urge our parents to applaud the whole team rather than just individuals; to clap all rather than just their own child. To congratulate every player at the end, not just their own child and his or her particular friends. Parents are overwhelmingly supportive although, of course, they might need the occasional reminder.

Five: Give players a voice

Finally, a child who feels able to voice their feelings and opinions feels valued, feels confident and feels successful. A group feedback session provides a great chance for our players to develop their voice. We will need to impose some sort of order – 'hands up before speaking' is perfect, because our players will be used to this from their schooling. Making sure that every child gets the chance to speak is vital; we may need to bring in quieter players by name, whilst never forcing them to speak if they do not want to. We react to their words positively. Similarly, we ensure that our parents do not shout down their children, at least within our setting.

The emotional, self-esteem based gains our players receive from acquiring and developing the benefits listed in this chapter will help not only their soccer, but their lives in general. That is something we all – parents, players and coaches – want. The atmosphere we create in our sessions and at our matches is the strongest tool for delivering these benefits. The most positive kind of atmosphere is best created through our, and our fellow coaches', demeanour. We are calm, relaxed, positive and encouraging. We do not shout; we do not criticise. We smile a lot. We keep our players busy. We are much more interested in our players' enjoyment and development than in winning. We rely on the support of our parents to spread the values we encourage. When our parents see that our interests are primarily in their children, they will be on our side.

Reward 3:

As a reward for completing this chapter, I'd like to offer you my free book on "Soccer Mental Toughness". It's a book on skills, strategies and exercises to use your mind to improve performances on the field. Just scan the QR code to get your book.

Conclusion

This has perhaps not been quite the usual manual for coaches. Whilst we have offered a range of drills, these – along with much of the remainder of the content – have focussed on age specific sessions and practices.

To summarise, in order to be the best coach that we can be for these young players, we need the following:

1. An understanding of child development. We must know the emotional, physical and cognitive limits of our players, to know from where they have come and to where they will be going as they get older. In brief, we can see child development as a continuum rather than a series of defined stages. The speed at which our players pass along that continuum is determined by a number of factors, most of which are out of our control. These include genetic factors, environmental factors, opportunities and social factors.

2. Extreme patience. We are, by definition, keen followers of soccer, and probably reasonably able and knowledgeable about the sport. It can be frustrating to work with young children who are so early in their soccer playing path, although it is also extremely rewarding to see the rapid progress they make.

3. Organisation. Sessions need to be busy with a rapid turnover of activities. Planning, preparing and running these can be challenging.

4. Creativity. Young children learn best through games and activities which are fun. These activities must also be directed at helping children's soccer playing knowledge, understanding, skills and techniques to improve.

5. Enthusiasm. Young children like energy. They have plenty of their own, and once underway can generate their own enthusiasm, but they often need a trigger, and this will most often come from the enthusiasm of their coach.

With these traits, however, anybody will become a successful and popular coach, one who delivers a huge amount to a young child's development, self-esteem and soccer playing potential. And they are wonderful gifts to bestow on a growing girl or boy.

The end... almost!

Reviews are not easy to come by.

As an independent author with a tiny marketing budget, I rely on readers, like you, to leave a short review on Amazon.

Even if it's just a sentence or two!

Thank you from the bottom of my heart for purchasing this book and reading it.